LOCAL OFFICIALS GUIDE TO

D1414985

THE COMMUNITY REINVESTMENT ACT

KF
1035
.M39
1991

Virginia M. Mayer
National League of Cities

Marina Sampanes
Carras Associates

James Carras
Carras Associates

Indiana University
Library
Northwest

NATIONAL LEAGUE OF CITIES

Copyright © 1991 by the

National League of Cities
Washington, D.C. 20004

ISBN 0-933729-64-2

NWST
IADJ 7190

CONTENTS

THE COMMUNITY REINVESTMENT ACT

FOREWORD

The major changes in the Community Reinvestment Act (CRA) that took effect in July 1990 give municipal officials significant new leverage to ensure that deposits in federally insured banking institutions are reinvested locally to meet housing and community development needs and goals.

The National League of Cities supported—and worked hard for—the changes in the Community Reinvestment Act, which made their way through Congress as part of the Financial Institutions Reform, Recovery, and Enforcement Act (FIRREA), better known as the savings and loan bailout. It is, in the League's estimation, one of the most important successes of the savings and loan bailout, and its passage is one of NLC's legislative successes.

The Community Reinvestment Act was originally enacted in 1977 to encourage banks to distribute loans equitably in all communities they serve. Enforcement, however, was inconsistent. The little reporting that was done was not made public but kept confidential.

The new law changes the system by which banks are rated for compliance with CRA and requires public disclosure of ratings, as well as written evaluations of a bank's performance in meeting community credit needs.

The changes give local officials an opportunity to take part in decisions affecting the investment of billions of dollars and they create an opportunity for public-private partnerships to rebuild neighborhoods in every municipality.

This *Local Officials Guide* to the Community Reinvestment Act provides a blueprint for building those partnerships. It explains the provisions of the legislation and its requirements in detail. It describes techniques for identifying economic development and housing needs, setting precise and measurable goals, and communicating those needs to the financial community. It also provides case studies of CRA policies and programs that are already working to improve neighborhoods across the country.

Acknowledgments

Credit for the NLC leadership goes to our Immediate Past President Bob Bolen, the Mayor of Fort Worth, Texas. His extraordinary efforts on behalf of all cities and towns were critical to providing these new tools in the law. So too, the guidance and leadership of Lee Cooke, Mayor of Austin, Texas, and Barbara Asher, councilmember of Atlanta, Georgia, the respective chairs of NLC's Finance, Administration, and Intergovernmental Affairs and Community and Economic Development policy committees, earn our appreciation and thanks.

The idea for this book emerged from discussions among NLC staff members Virginia Mayer, Bill Barnes, and Frank Shafroth. Their strong belief in the importance of CRA as a vital tool for cities and towns was the driving force behind this publication, a series of articles in Nation's Cities Weekly and a set of training seminars for local officials.

Virginia Mayer served as project director for this publication, nurturing it from a concept in a few people's heads to the comprehensive and practical guidebook that you have before you. NLC contracted with Carras Associates, a development finance consulting firm with offices in Boston, Massachusetts and Fort Lauderdale, Florida to help write the guidebook.

The principal authors are Marina E. Sampanes, senior associate, Carras Associates, Virginia Mayer, and James Carras, president, Carras Associates. The case studies in Chapter Four were written by Bridget Ware, an associate with Carras Associates. The programs in Chapter Five were written by Laura

Duenes, associate with Carras Associate. General research report was given by Jennifer Kelley Reed, associate with Carras Associates.

Many others contributed their time, expertise and support for which we owe much gratitude. Bill Barnes and Frank Shafroth provided invaluable expertise, support and vision throughout the project. Clint Page edited and produced this guidebook. Jeff Fletcher assisted with the design and production of the book. The cover art was produced by Robinson, Pritchard and Boyer.

We are grateful to those who reviewed the publication and provided valuable comments, including Thom McCloud, director, NLC's Public Affairs Center; Sandi Braunstein and Ken Fain of the Federal Reserve Bank; Chris Lindley, deputy mayor, Rochester, New York; Wes Pratt, councilmember, San Diego, California; Daniel Tabor, councilmember, Inglewood, California; and Carol Robbins, principal, PlanComm Consulting.

We would also like to thank the public and private sector leaders featured in the programs and case studies found in this book. We salute their creativity, energy and commitment which have resulted not only in successful public-private partnerships but critical reinvestment in our cities and towns.

Donald J. Borut
Executive Director
National League of Cities

Reinvesting in America's Home Towns: The Local Official's Guide to the Community Reinvestment Act

D o you want to stimulate a flow of investment capital that can build housing, restore neighborhoods, and revitalize commercial districts in your city?

Of course you do. Any local official would. And virtually any city or town can, thanks to changes in the Community Reinvestment Act (CRA) that took effect in July 1990. CRA creates a significant opportunity for local officials to make sure that deposits in federally insured banking institutions are reinvested in the communities the banks serve. The potential reinvestment in housing, community and economic development far exceeds any potential federal assistance to cities and towns.

Through provisions of the Act, for example, Boston helped secure an approximately $400 million commitment from Massachusetts bankers that will leverage up to $1 billion of new investment statewide, including as much as $400 million in the city.

West Hollywood, California, used CRA provisions to help secure the participation of local lenders in small business development, affordable housing, and bank services for the city's sizable elderly population.

These examples, and many others described elsewhere in this *Local Officials Guide,* show that the Community Reinvestment Act does more than set certain requirements for banks. It does that, of course, but for local governments it creates a powerful opportunity — the opportunity to forge public-private partnerships to rebuild neighborhoods. But like any opportunity, this opportunity requires action on your part to make it pay off.

This *Local Officials Guide* can help you seize the opportunity, understand the CRA, and increase its impact on your city.

Local governments are on the front lines in the battle to preserve and build the economic vitality of their communities. Capital is a critical ingredient in local economic development, and leveraging bank investment in urban, rural, and inner-city communities is critical to the effective use of capital.

In the Community Reinvestment Act, city officials have a unique opportunity to exercise their leadership and build affordable housing and economic development partnerships with local financial institutions. The National League of Cities has long recognized the value of the CRA and has consistently supported the enforcement and strengthening of this important tool.

History of CRA

The relatively brief history of the CRA is one of ebb and flow. During the 1970s, community groups and politicians formed a strong alliance around the issue of urban disinvestment. This coalition was deeply disturbed that financial institutions, by redlining many low- and moderate-income neighborhoods, were ignoring the obligations to which they committed when they accepted their public charters. The concern became so forceful in the late 1970s that Congress passed special legislation — the Community Reinvestment Act — requiring federal regulators to examine financial institutions' efforts to meet the credit and bank service needs of their communities.

To ensure compliance with CRA procedural requirements and substantive performance standards, bank regulatory agencies created twelve assessment factors, grouped in five categories:

- Ascertaining community credit needs;
- Marketing of products and services to the entire community;
- Opening and closing of branches and geographic distribution of loans and services;
- Origination of various types of loans in the bank's community and discriminatory activities; and
- Community development.

While the Community Reinvestment Act of 1977 was an important first step toward increasing bank accountability to low- and moderate-income communities, its early effectiveness was limited. The past three years, however, have witnessed a rising tide of renewed attention to the CRA by Congress, bank regulators, city governments, and community-based organizations. Several factors account for this increased interest:

- The significant decrease in federal programs serving economically disadvantaged neighborhoods;
- The advent of interstate banking, generating an increased number of merger applications subject to public comment (e.g., "CRA Protests");
- The shifting real estate markets;
- The failure of numerous federally-insured financial institutions (savings and loan associations, in particular);
- Increased public and press scrutiny of bank lending practices, especially to minority neighborhoods;
- Increased Congressional oversight;
- Increased regulatory enforcement of CRA; and
- Public disclosure of a new CRA ratings system.

These trends converged in the federal legislation of 1989. The revised CRA presents local communities with an opportunity to leverage and maximize the benefits of the Community Reinvestment Act. Financial institutions are looking for ways to comply with the CRA, identify new market opportunities, and cultivate community goodwill. Many lenders, however, fear that "CRA lending" is a losing proposition. Few are technically skilled in community development lending, which often requires use of government and alternative resources. In increasing numbers, they are turning to local government for community insights and program ideas. Elected and appointed officials and representatives in both the policy and programmatic areas may now find themselves with an audience of inquisitive bankers, seeking information for their credit needs assessments, on activities in which they can participate, and on their institution's record of community involvement.

Local officials must be prepared for such queries — not just with facts, but with attitudes and ideas that can actually engage banks in community revitalization. Governments must understand the needs of their low- and moderate-income residents, decide what the city wants from banks, and define a plan for action and for partnership. That requires meticulous fact-finding and carefully set, coherent priorities and goals.

The law is self-enforcing. It does not require any bank to take any action. It allows banks to work in any number of ways with a city or town to receive an excellent rating. But without the efforts of local elected officials, the law is unlikely to lead to any change in your community.

Many elements contribute to the success of a community investment strategy, but communication among and commitment from all sectors are the most critical. Each group has its own agenda: financial institutions, while facing difficult economic times, are most concerned about complying with the CRA with minimal risk; community-based organizations desperately need support for their activities in light of limited government and private resources; and local government is concerned with the development and maintenance of the economic vitality and growth of its communities with dwindling financial resources.

As lenders sort out how CRA procedural requirements and direction apply to them, local officials must assess past bank lending activities in low- and moderate-income areas and plan for future activities. It is up to local government officials to uncover the intersections of interests. City officials must explore and assume appropriate roles as advocates, facilitators, brokers, resource providers, architects of comprehensive community investment programs, and — above all — proactive partners in the process of long-term programs and investments.

This *Local Officials Guide* provides information and step-by-step instructions for marshalling resources from local lenders for the low- and moderate-income areas of your community. It presents

■ an arsenal of information on the Community Reinvestment Act;

■ an understanding of the responsibilities of financial institutions;

■ descriptions and examples of roles that local government leaders can play to increase private investment in their communities; and

■ new partnerships and programs that may emerge from the CRA process.

Chapter One reviews the CRA, identifies the major tenets of the newly strengthened CRA and the tools that can be used by local governments.

Chapter Two shows the steps a city government should take towards establishing a comprehensive community investment strategy.

Chapter Three describes techniques for evaluating the activities of lenders in your community.

Chapter Four looks at examples of how officials in two cities have used CRA to increase investment in their low- and moderate-income communities.

Chapter Five provides further specific tools and strategies for application in your community, through descriptive case studies of partnership efforts, including model programs and vehicles.

The Appendices include:

- Appendix A: the text of the Community Reinvestment Act,
- Appendix B: the text of the Joint CRA Policy Statment of 1989,
- Appendix C: the text of the New Uniform Guidelines and CRA Rating System,
- Appendix D: the addresses of the federal regulatory agencies that enforce the Act's requirements, and
- Appendix E: a chart detailing the CRA rating system.

This *Local Officials Guide* is based on the conviction that local government can and should shape the financial future of its community. The Community Reinvestment Act is a tool that cities can use to increase bank involvement in affordable housing, small and minority business development, and more accessible bank services. With the assistance of this Guide, your city government can take a leadership role in creating a dynamic partnership with local financial institutions to support what you are already doing or plan to do to meet the needs of your community.

CHAPTER ONE

CRA –
The Law and the Politics

The Community Reinvestment Act, commonly known as the CRA, was enacted as Title VIII of the Housing and Community Development Act of 1977. Its passage was the culmination of years of grassroots community activism, research, and regulatory protest dealing with bank lending practices in cities around the country. Financial institutions in Chicago, Cleveland, New York, Boston, Baltimore, and other cities were accused of "redlining," or refusing to make mortgage loans in lower-income, often minority, inner-city neighborhoods.

The vigorous community and activist scrutiny of the banking industry led the Senate to hold hearings to investigate the redlining allegations and determine if the industry was discriminating against certain communities. During the course of the hearings, Congress was told that bank disinvestment, coupled with a decline of basic services such as transportation, health care, public safety, and retail stores, intensified the decline of older urban neighborhoods. This trend of large-scale disinvestment and shifts in racial and ethnic mix heightened the urgency for financial institutions to ensure that they meet the banking needs of their communities.

The Community Reinvestment Act reinforced the message, spelled out in bank charters, that federally insured and regulated financial institutions have the inherent obligation to meet the convenience and needs of their communities. The CRA reinforced this basic tenet and required that financial institutions not only meet depository needs but also credit needs of local communities, including low- and moderate-income communities (see box below). The CRA applies to all federally chartered and insured depository institutions: bank holding companies, national banks, savings and loan associations, and federal savings banks (all referred to as "banks" in this book). In addition, some twenty states have developed similar CRA statutes.

The CRA gave communities the opportunity to help modify bank lending practices. The law encouraged every bank to identify the credit needs of its community, including low- and moderate-income neighborhoods; develop or adapt products to respond to those needs; and market the services to those communities.

While the CRA was a helpful first step toward increasing bank investment in low- and moderate-income communities, several problems limited its effectiveness: the language was

---

The Community Reinvestment Act

The CRA, enacted in 1977, requires each federal financial supervisory agency to use its authority when conducting examinations to encourage the financial institutions it supervises to help meet the credit needs of the community. Specifically, a regulatory agency conducting an examination of a financial institution must:

(1) assess the institution's record of meeting the credit needs of its entire community, including low- and moderate income neighborhoods, consistent with the safe and sound operation of the institution; and

(2) take that record into account in evaluating an application for a charter, deposit insurance, branch or other deposit facility, office relocation, merger, or holding company acquisition of a depository institution. 12 U.S.C. § 2903

Simply stated, the CRA and the implementing regulations place upon all financial institutions an affirmative responsibility to treat the credit needs of low- and moderate income memebers of their communities as they would treat any other market for services that the bank has decided to serve. As with any other targeted market, financial institutions are expected to ascertain credit needs and demonstrate their response to those needs.

Source: Joint Policy Statement

vague, giving few specific guidelines; the law had no teeth – there were no concrete incentives for complying and no immediate penalties for not complying; and scrutiny and enforcement were often lax. In an effort to spur full enforcement of the act, community-based organizations and coalitions challenged or protested bank applications for mergers, acquisitions, and branch openings. Since 1985, with the advent of interstate banking, community organizations used the regulatory system to leverage more than two hundred lending agreements, most of them with large regional banking institutions. These agreements spelled out specific commitments for mortgages, affordable housing, and small business lending.

Two factors brought renewed attention to the CRA in the late 1980s. The lack of federal funds for affordable housing and community development forced local development agencies and community-based organizations to intensify their search for private financing resources. In their efforts to gain financing, they often used CRA as a leveraging tool to encourage bank participation in community investment programs and partnerships. During the same years, new studies of bank lending patterns in several major cities, alleging that redlining and discriminatory practices continued to exist, received extraordinary press coverage (for example, in Atlanta, Boston, Detroit, and New York). The renewed public focus on investment practices resulted in an important regulatory policy statement in March 1989, and then in August 1989, in new legislation that increased the enforcement and power of CRA.

Federal Regulators' Statement on CRA

In March, 1989, the four federal bank regulatory agencies – the Federal Reserve Board, the Federal Home Loan Bank Board (since replaced by the Office of Thrift Supervision), the Office of the Comptroller of the Currency, and the Federal Deposit Insurance Corporation – issued a Joint Statement on the Community Reinvestment Act to clarify the responsibilities of banks and community-based organizations. The significance of this policy statement extends beyond the printed words. It was the first comment by regulators on the CRA since a brief informational statement in 1980.

The document was carefully crafted to detail regulatory expectations and guidelines to both financial institutions and their communities. The twenty-three-page Joint CRA Statement (see Appendix B) details:

- the basic components of an effective bank CRA policy;
- the need for periodic review and documentation by lenders of their CRA performance (use of expanded CRA statements); and
- the need for ongoing communication with community organizations.

The Statement noted that all federally regulated financial institutions (referred to as "banks" throughout this book) must be far more proactive in communicating with their low- and moderate-income communities and "assessing their credit needs." In other words, financial institutions must have a better understanding of their communities' credit needs, resources, and concerns — and banks must respond to these needs with responsive loan products and programs. Effectively, banks need to look at the CRA from a strategic point of view and develop a plan of action.

Components of an Effective Bank CRA Policy

A bank's CRA Statement, available to the public by law, generally outlines the description of its lending community and the types of credit offered (see box on page 11). In their 1989 policy, the regulators encouraged financial institutions to expand their CRA Statements to elaborate on CRA efforts and describe their CRA performance, including:

- the methods and results of ascertaining the community credit needs;

- steps taken to meet the needs, such as special credit-related programs, educational or technical assistance programs; and
- descriptions of their outreach, product development, and marketing efforts, plus a summary documenting their results.

The regulators also recommended including a summary of the results of the bank's Internal CRA Review. Such documentation in the CRA Statement serves as the framework for public comment on an institution's CRA performance. American Security Bank of Washington, D.C., and Bank of America,

---

CRA Statements of Financial Institutions

CRA Statements describe the financial institution, its community, and the products and services offered. Federal regulators strongly encourage financial institutions to expand the contents of these Statements, which are reviewed by bank management on an annual basis. CRA Statements must be available to the public at all branch locations.

Cities should review the CRA Statements of local banks and thrifts to keep informed of how the institutions view themselves and what they are doing in the community. Basic elements of a CRA Statement include:

Description of the financial institution and its branches;
Delineation of its community (with a map) and how it was determined;
List of specific types of credit and services the institution is prepared to extend within each community;
Copy of its CRA Notice;
Minutes of the Board meeting in which the Statement was approved.

In addition, an expanded CRA Statement may include the following:

Methods used in ascertaining community credit needs;
Results of the credit needs assessment process;
Steps taken to meet identified credit needs;
Special programs (i.e., educational or technical assistance)
Community outreach efforts;
Product development efforts;
Marketing techniques to reach low- and moderate-income communities;
Results of the institution's Internal CRA Review;
Community development projects in which it is involved;
Community leadership activities with community-based development organizations;
Charitable contributions to support community-based activities for low- and moderate-income communities.

California, have expanded CRA Statements that can serve as models for other institutions. The CRA Statement may be a good first step to learning of the activities and community philosophy of each bank. A note of caution: not all banks have expanded their CRA statements, which may indicate a lack of awareness on their part.

Bank/Community Relationships

The most effective community investment initiatives have come from discussions among lenders, local government, and community groups. In many cases, these discussions or negotiations have resulted from either challenges to bank expansion applications or publicized mortgage lending studies done by grassroots community advocates and coalitions.

The Joint CRA Statement encourages banks and community groups to engage in dialogue and establish ongoing relationships without the acrimony of past CRA protests of bank applications for mergers or acquisitions. Interested parties, such as city governments and community groups, are "strongly encouraged" to comment on bank performance and to bring their concerns and issues "to the attention of the institution and its supervisory agency at the earliest possible time."

One method of communicating concerns to a bank is to use the bank's Public Comment File. Banks must maintain a Public Comment File containing any CRA statements in effect during the past two years, a copy of the most recent CRA Performance Evaluation (conducted on and after July 1, 1990), and all comments on bank performance; copies must be sent to the appropriate federal agencies. This file is open for public review. More details on using the public comment process are given in Chapter Three.

Financial Institutions Reform, Recovery, and Enforcement Act of 1989 (FIRREA)

In August 1989, five months after the regulatory statement was issued, Congress passed the Federal Institutions Reform, Recovery, and Enforcement Act (FIRREA), focusing attention on its role in restructuring the nation's thrift industry and the cost to taxpayers. The hefty document also included new CRA disclosure provisions that could have a profound impact on communities around the country and their quests for increased bank involvement in their minority and low- and moderate-income neighborhoods. FIRREA amended the CRA and the Home Mortgage Disclosure Act (HMDA) to increase the amount of information available to the public by

- revising the CRA rating system,
- requiring disclosure of CRA ratings and evaluations, and
- expanding HMDA reporting requirements.

New CRA Rating System

The regulators use twelve assessment factors to review bank CRA performance. Appendix E gives a detailed description of these assessment factors. The CRA assessment factors are grouped into five performance categories:

- **Ascertainment of community credit needs:** activities conducted by the institution to determine the credit needs of the community, including efforts to communicate with the community about credit services, and the extent to which the institution's board of directors participates in formulating policies and reviewing performance with repsect to the purposes of the CRA.

■ **Marketing and types of credit offered and extended:** the extent of marketing and special credit-related programs to make members of the community aware of the bank's credit services; orgination of residential mortgage loans, housing rehabilitation loans, small business or small farm loans, and rural development loans, or the purchase of such loans originated in the community; participation in governmentally insured, guaranteed or subsidized loans programs for housing, small businesses, or small farms.

■ **Geographic distribution and record of opening and closing offices:** geographic distribution of credit extensions, credit applications, and credit denials; the record of opening and closing offices and providing services.

■ **Discrimination and other illegal credit practices:** any practices to discourage applications for types of credit set forth in the bank's CRA statement; evidence of prohibited discriminatory or other illegal credit practices.

■ **Community development:** participation, including investments, in local community development and redevelopment projects or programs; ability to help meet community credit needs based on its financial condition and size, legal impediments, local economic conditions, and other factors; any other facts that bear upon the extent to which the bank is helping meet community credit needs.

In the past, banks received a numerical rating for each of the five categories, from which a composite rating (from one, the best, to five, the worst) was derived. The grading criteria for each category were not specific, and the weighted value of each category in relation to the composite rating was not clear. The lax enforcement of CRA was demonstrated as the composite ratings tended not to reflect much analysis; virtually every institution received a passing grade. Less than 3 percent of all banks received less than passing grades. The regulatory agency's evaluation process and ratings for each institution were not publicly disclosed.

The FIRREA amendments changed the grading system to replace the earlier numerical scale with a four-tier descriptive rating system. The new ratings are:

- Outstanding record of meeting community credit needs
- Satisfactory record of meeting community credit needs
- Needs to Improve record of meeting community credit needs
- Substantial Non-compliance in meeting community credit needs

All four regulatory agencies now use this uniform set of CRA disclosure guidelines and the same rating system. These new guidelines provide consistent and better defined parameters

---

CRA Ratings Go Public Under FIRREA

As of July 1, 1990, CRA ratings are no longer on a numerical basis; rather they are written evaluations using a four-tier descriptive system:

Outstanding record of meeting community credit needs
Satisfactory record of meeting community credit needs
Needs to improve record of meeting community credit needs
Substantial noncompliance in meeting community credit needs

Each financial institution will have its performance reviewed in five major categories:

1. Ascertainment of community credit needs;
2. Marketing and types of credit extended;
3. Geographical distribution and record of opening and closing offices;
4. Discrimination and other illegal credit practices; and,
5. Community development.

An "outstanding" rating will be achieved only by financial institutions that demonstrate certain qualities, including leadership in ascertaining community needs, participation in community revitalization, and affirmative involvement in planning, implementing, and monitoring their CRA-related performance. Most CRA observers agree that "outstanding" ratings will be difficult to achieve.

CRA Evaluations can be found at an institution's main office and designated branch in each of its local communities. They are not, however, required to provide free copies.

for the new ratings. For example, CRA evaluations now include findings and supporting facts for each category, as well as overall conclusions. In addition to being more qualitative, the ratings are now disclosed to the public.

Disclosure of CRA Ratings and Evaluations

The new disclosure policy created by FIRREA is important to city officials because it provides a new tool for increasing bank community investment. Under the new regulations, lenders are required to make the CRA evaluations public within thirty business days of their receipt from the regulator. The evaluation must be placed in a financial institution's CRA public file at its main office, and also at one designated office in each community it serves. It must be made available to anyone who requests the information. The institution may also include its response to the evaluation in the public comment file, if it so chooses.

Expansion of the Home Mortgage Disclosure Act

The Home Mortgage Disclosure Act was passed in 1975, early in the debate over redlining, to create a national system under which regulated financial institutions were to report mortgage loans.

The lack of home mortgage availability, especially in urban areas, resulted in charges of discrimination or "redlining," the systematic exclusion of certain geographic areas as viable communities for bank investment. The allegations of redlining centered around minority communities. Community leaders used creative but elementary means to demonstrate bank disinvestment through maps of neighborhoods marked where mortgages had been made. Lenders had no systematic method to indicate where specific mortgages had been made. Early in the debate, the Home Mortgage Disclosure Act (HMDA) emerged. HMDA instituted a national reporting system of mortgage loans by regulated financial institutions.

HMDA required financial institutions to disclose information on their mortgage originations and purchases. Banks were required to submit summary reports of their mortgage loan activity by geographic area. The reports, however, lacked detail in reporting information to reflect loan activity with respect to expressed demand (loan applications). Also, rapid investment in lower-income communities often resulted in gentrification, displacing residents for newer, more affluent buyers and investors. Financing for gentrification alone does not fulfill institutions' obligations under the Community Reinvestment Act.

HMDA's limited effectiveness as an analytical tool resulted in efforts to amend the Act. Eventually, changes to the HMDA were implemented through the Financial Institutions Reform, Recovery, and Enforcement Act (FIRREA) of 1989. The changes to HMDA will make it a valuable tool for cities and towns as they define their community needs.

Reporting Requirements

HMDA now requires financial institutions to disclose the race, gender, and income level of all applicants as well as borrowers by census tract. Institutions must also report on the disposition of each loan request and may, if they choose, indicate the reason if the application is denied. Loans sold to the secondary market must be noted according to the category of purchaser.

The first set of expanded reports is due to the supervisory agencies by March 1, 1991. Each agency, in turn, gives the data to the Federal Reserve, which will produce a series of data tables for each reporting institution. Each bank's report will be sent to the bank; the bank will subsequently make the report available to the public upon request. As in the past, the regulators will also continue to provide these reports to local HMDA depositories in each metropolitan statistical area, where copies of the HMDA data for each local institution are available for inspection or copying by the public.

These reporting requirements extend to virtually all mortgage lenders, including mortgage and home finance companies, banks, savings and loans, and credit unions. The only financial institutions exempt from these new requirements are those with assets of less than $30 million (including assets of the parent organization). In addition, the U.S. Department of Housing and Urban Development (HUD) requires all FHA lenders, regardless of size or affiliation, to comply with the new HMDA requirements. FHA lenders must report HMDA data on all FHA activity to HUD, regardless of reporting to any other regulatory agency.

Bank Activities/Responses Encouraged by Regulators

In their 1989 statement and their subsequent actions, the regulatory agencies have encouraged financial institutions to undertake many activities in their banking and CRA efforts. A more complete list is given in Chapter Two, but in general, the following actions are encouraged:

- Participate in various government-insured lending programs and other types of lending programs, such as conventional mortgage loans with private mortgage insurance to help meet identified credit needs.
- Develop and advertise services to benefit low- and moderate-income persons, such as government check cashing and low-cost checking accounts.
- Target an advertising and marketing strategy to inform low- and moderate income groups of the loan and deposit services available to them. Identify means to reach these groups (for example, small newspapers, radio, television, community/church organizations, non-English literature).
- Establish a process involving all levels of management in efforts to contact governmental leaders, economic development practitioners, businesses and business as-

sociations, and community organizations to discuss the financial services that are needed by the community.

- Participate and provide assistance to community development programs and projects.
- Invest in state and municipal bonds.

Some bankers need to be reminded that CRA-related loans and activities are safe and sound investments in the community. The agencies discourage "give-away programs" that would place an institution at undue risk—and they offer many approaches lenders can take to address community credit needs. City government should evaluate local lenders' CRA programs using their own criteria. Chapter Two illustrates how to define your community credit needs. Chapter Three details the process for evaluating local lenders' CRA programs.

CRA evaluations for all CRA examinations commenced by bank regulatory agencies after July 1, 1990 will be made public. This is a large number of evaluations, and it will take some time before evaluations for all banks are available. As examinations are completed, the public evaluations will be sent to the banks by the regulatory agency. The bank will then have thirty business days in which to release the evaluation to the public.

To determine whether a particular bank's CRA Evaluation is available to the public, contact the bank directly or consult the bank's primary supervisory agency. Each supervisory agency now periodically publishes lists of those banks for which public CRA evaluations are available. The addresses for the regulatory agencies are listed in Appendix D.

The New CRA Environment

The efforts by community organizations to change policy to mandate public disclosure of CRA ratings were opposed by the banking industry. Proponents for public disclosure (community organizations, state and local governments, and the National League of Cities) say such information will be helpful in several ways.

- Disclosure places pressure on regulators to make their examinations more thorough.
- Public disclosure provides communities with more information and encourages banks to be more active.
- Disclosure will make CRA efforts a more competitive element among local lenders.
- Lenders with solid CRA programs will be duly noted and can promote their record.
- The descriptive information in the evaluation identifies the strengths and weaknesses of an institution's CRA program and policies.
- The public can assess its impact on the financial institutions' CRA policies.
- Access to such information indicates the emphasis on and interpretation of certain elements of CRA by the supervisory agencies.

In opposing public disclosure, the banking industry claimed that ratings could be misinterpreted by consumers (possibly confusing CRA with safety and soundness evaluations, which are not disclosed publicly) or misrepresented by others to cast aspersions on an institution's community record.

As more examinations are released, it seems certain that some financial institutions will incorporate them into public relations and marketing strategies. For instance, Bank of America in California, which was rated "outstanding," issued a press release and aggressively distributed copies of its examination findings. The public may request a meeting with the regulators and place letters to financial institutions in their public comment files (with copies sent to the regulatory agencies) prior to the anticipated examinations. All of the effects of public disclosure have yet to be seen, however.

What the New CRA Environment Means Locally

The new CRA environment spells opportunity. It also means more information, more communication, and more collaboration among the public, private, and nonprofit sectors.

Implications for Lenders

Many lenders must now respond to the new CRA environment. Lenders are seeking to minimize the politicizing of the CRA issue by institutionalizing community reinvestment practices as a normal course of business. This is accomplished through aggressive community outreach that facilitates dialogue and that can in turn help identify and take advantage of sound market opportunities. A receptive bank attitude fosters goodwill and cooperation between the lending institution and its community. All this can result in good business for the lender and economic growth and vitality for its community. As the First National Bank of Chicago discovered, a neighborhood lending operation can be a strong profit center.

Local officials who give increased attention to the CRA, however, should view it in the context of today's uncertain economic climate and the banking industry's losses, especially in real estate lending. The declining financial condition of many institutions has increased federal regulators' scrutiny of loans. In turn, lenders have reduced all types of lending. As a result, many lenders feel they are receiving mixed signals from regulators who are, on one hand, scrutinizing all lending and, on the other hand, encouraging banks to undertake community development lending. Though the two are not mutually exclusive, this environment appears to be somewhat confusing for lenders.

Implications for Local Governments

Together, the CRA Policy Statement, increased regulatory enforcement, and disclosure of CRA ratings and HMDA information provide new tools to help local governments and community organizations make sure that financial institutions invest in low- and moderate-income areas.

The need for ongoing dialogue across the interested sectors is an obvious part of identifying needs and developing responses to those needs. Local government officials can establish a constructive process to work on community reinvestment issues with local lenders and community representatives. Local government and the lenders share the mutual interests of complying with federal regulations while building the local economy and community development base. Armed with more complete information on local lenders' performance and a local credit needs assessment, city officials can work confidently with the banking community on specific issues affecting targeted low- and moderate-income neighborhoods.

The Role of Local Officials

Often, public offices, functions, and programs are generalized under the catch-all category of "government." Different government interests identify priorities, needs, and solutions based on their respective interest or expertise. For instance, the priority "development" issues of the Mayor may differ from the immediate concerns of the City Council, while the Planning and Community Development Departments may be focusing on different phases and elements of the community economic development process. Government is always blending political agendas with planning, policy, and programmatic policies. It is important, however, not to send mixed messages to residents, banks, and other interests. Making sure that all parties are working under the same message is a key element in success.

Notwithstanding the different perspectives, functions and concerns, city leaders need to take advantage of the current CRA climate by assuming a variety of roles. Leadership takes many forms, depending on the local personalities and political climate of the community.

City as Advocate

City officials can be the advocates for community reinvestment, raising the credit issues that need to be addressed by financial institutions. The city can increase awareness of the need for investment initiatives through studies, such as a community credit needs assessment and/or analysis of HMDA data; planning documents; public hearings on issues; and community meetings. The city can provide uniform demographic data to all financial institutions so that all are working from the same base when they develop their plans. As an advocate, the city should be prepared to ask the questions and exert pressure on local financial institutions to respond to the community credit needs.

City as Architect

The city may also choose to be the architect of a comprehensive community investment strategy or specific program. With the needs of the community identified, the city can develop an investment strategy that maximizes the city resources by investing with private sector actors. Get a head start by formalizing the goals, objectives, and potential responses discussed within local government. Through these efforts, the city sets the agenda and framework for discussion. The resulting strategy or plan can be the basis for discussion with local lenders and community-based organizations.

City as Facilitator

City leaders can serve as the facilitators and brokers, building bridges between the local financial institutions and community-based organizations and building consensus based on common interests. The city assumes this role by sponsoring hearings, forums, and smaller meetings among interested parties. Community-based organizations know what their needs are, and the financial institutions need to understand them. The education that comes from discussion among the public, private, and non-profit sectors helps construct a community investment program that is doable and beneficial. As facilitator, the city can build consensus among groups with very different perspectives.

City as Provider

Local government can be the provider, as well, of public resources to be used with new bank commitments to increase their impact and reduce the risk for private lenders. Such participation can include loan guarantees, loan programs, loan participations, technical assistance services, and community outreach.

City as Partner

Most important, in all situations, and along with any other roles it may take on, the city can be a partner in the development and implementation of a comprehensive community investment program. Working with all interested groups, the city can establish a process, participate in the process, and help get a community investment program off the drawing board and into the community. Local officials can help create new vehicles and intermediaries that facilitate bank participation in community economic development.

Prepare for Your Roles

Whatever role or roles the city chooses to assume, the greatest success will occur when city officials are prepared. Being prepared in the following areas can demonstrate the local government's leadership in the community reinvestment process.

■ **Get the facts.** Know your community and its credit needs.

- **Set the Agenda.** Armed with the knowledge of the needs in the community, local officials should identify their goals and plans for the city. Specific projects in which participation by the private sector can leverage precious public dollars can be used as the initial areas of focus for discussion with local lenders.
- **Dedicate Staff Time.** As with any city plan or program development, consider committing staff time to working on this process in two areas: meetings with local lenders and community organizations; and program/product development to consider for your city.
- **Research Product and Vehicle Options.** Financing products require creativity and resourcefulness. Learn what is working and what has not worked elsewhere; explore initiatives in other communities. The National League of Cities can serve as a peer-to-peer referral resource for local officials interested in learning from colleagues in other areas.

Community Credit Needs Assessments and Strategic Planning

Given today's shifting economic and regulatory environment, cities and towns are constantly reevaluating their resources to most efficiently meet community needs. The Community Reinvestment Act gives local governments a way to bring banks into a strategic planning process for community investment. Creativity and cooperation are vital to the success of these efforts. Cooperation must extend across government departments and agencies. Before any investment plan can be developed, however, the city or town must understand the basic needs and capital requirements for housing and economic and community development in targeted low- and moderate-income areas.

In short, you must know what your needs are before you sit down with the bankers. That's what a community credit needs assessment is all about.

The community reinvestment plan that grows out of this effort provides a menu from which local banks can select ways to fulfill CRA requirements and meet the credit and banking needs of the community.

Understanding the Credit Needs of the Community

Ascertaining the credit needs of a bank's delineated community is the first step and an integral part of an effective CRA process. An ongoing credit needs assessment is the backbone of any effective program. It is also one of the assessment factors used to evaluate a lender's record. Banks are expected to, or should be prepared to, respond to the needs identified in their assessment process if they want to get good ratings from the examiners.

You need information to back up your claims of credit gaps. A needs assessment, similar to a market study, provides the statistical and qualitative analysis needed to substantiate community credit and bank service needs in your target areas. The data analysis and resulting conclusions from a needs assessment further encourages the various parties to work towards developing new or adapting old programs.

Different organizations conduct needs assessments for different reasons. Banks do so because the CRA requires them to ascertain the credit needs of their communities, including low- and moderate-income communities. City government agencies identify needs for their community and economic development programs. Community-based organizations survey the needs of their constituencies for the issues they face and the services they need. But the comprehensive analyses of community credit needs that mesh the views of financial institutions, city, and community-based organizations on housing, community, and economic development issues as they relate to capital are typically not found in most communities.

The credit needs assessment is the precursor of a bank's and a community's CRA program. The needs assessment can provide an agreed-upon set of community facts and unveil issues and potential resources for addressing them. The needs identified provide the targets for designing a sound and appropriate action plan for investing in low- and moderate-income communities.

Credit needs assessments can be conducted in a number of ways. Banks can do them individually or collectively. Outside parties can conduct the assessments for an organization or a group of organizations. In some cases, local governments have conducted community credit needs assessments. But regardless of who actually carries out the assessment, a thorough community credit needs assessment should have input from all interests. And even more important, the fact that an outside party is doing a credit needs assessment should not preclude the city's doing one — and vice versa.

The banks' efforts should be proactive and on-going, continually reaching out to local governments, businesses, community organizations, and community residents. While these efforts *should* happen, local government officials need to determine how to make sure they *do* happen. Particular attention should be given to the low- and moderate-income areas. To determine needs, a bank may use mail and telephone surveys, focus groups, and community meetings. An institution may choose to establish a community advisory council, consisting of city officials, community representatives, and small and minority business owners, among others. The community advisory council's advice can, in part, provide a basis for product and service development. Council meetings and correspondence should be well documented.

Often, the process results in a printed study for one institution or a group of institutions. These reports benefit more organizations than just financial institutions. In fact, regulatory agencies, community-based organizations, city agencies, and other groups conduct these assessments to articulate financing concerns and better understand their communities.

This chapter outlines the process and examines the information necessary for a thorough community credit needs assessment.

Conducting a Community Credit Needs Assessment

A thorough community credit needs assessment should contain detailed demographic information, housing data and conditions, and the economic environment of a community. With information on these broad categories, local officials can draw specific and general short- and long-term conclusions about the community's financing needs. Data should be gathered on the census tract level or for even smaller areas whenever possible. Description on a neighborhood basis rather than on a community-wide basis can help target programs more effectively. In this way, the credit needs assessment will demonstrate the varying conditions among neighborhoods.

It is important to inform the lending community of your initiative early in the process and invite them to participate in the process (more on this later in the chapter). Their input will assist in developing viable community investment strategies. This step formalizes the relationship with the financial institution and paves the way for a working relationship.

It is important, also, to set a realistic schedule for carrying out a community needs assessment; the steps are described in the box on page 31. A rough schedule might look like this:

Task	Time
Community credit needs assessment and financial analysis	2 - 3 months
Setting precise and measurable goals	1 - 2 months
Development of community investment plan	2 - 4 months

Some of these tasks can be done concurrently; the credit needs assessment and financial market analysis can take place at the same time. As issues emerge, identification of goals can be developed. Much depends on the resources allocated to conducting the actual work and the time committed to these efforts. Establishing reasonable, somewhat aggressive goals, recommendations, and time lines will place the city in a leadership position for the process of completing the community credit needs assessment, which will feed directly into development of a Community Investment Plan.

Steps to a Community Credit Needs Assessment

Needs assessments substantiate credit and banking needs of a community. The information provided in the needs assessment can be used to leverage resources from otherwise reluctant sources. Follow the steps below to determine the credit needs of community residents, community-based organizations, and businesses.

1. Meet with the Community

Survey and interview identified contacts to determine credit needs of target population and community where located. Those to contact include civic organizations, business leaders, community-based organizations, community advocates, population focus groups, trade associations, and nonprofit developers. Identify and describe all key public and private actors in community and economic development efforts.

2. Collect and Compile Data

Collect pertinent data on population, income, housing, and economic indicators from local public agencies, state agencies, private data companies, libraries, chambers of commerce, real estate boards, etc.

3. Analyze the Financial Market

Identify sources of capital for affordable housing development and rehabilitation, small and minority business development, and community-based organizations. Identify financial imtermediaries that could provide capital. Evaluate local lending institutions' compliance with CRA goals. Ask the regulatory agencies for application notices. Review business and financial publications to keep current on the status of the financial industry. Evaluate the availability and potential impact of the capital sources you have identified.

4. Document the Results

Prepare a final written document analyzing the results of collected data and surveys. The document details the credit needs of the community, with particular attention to the needs of low-income people and community-based organizations. The final report also recommends solutions to identified needs and serves as a planning and resource document for a partnership effort.

Meet with the Community

Develop a detailed profile or description of the area intended to be the focus of community investment activity. This description should include community characteristics such as population demographics, housing conditions, commercial areas, and any other community resources. Compiling this information helps the city determine the general direction the community investment program should take. It also outlines the basic needs of the community in terms of issues — homeownership versus rental housing, for example, or commercial area revitalization.

Determine if initiatives are underway or expected that could affect the target area and its residents. Ascertain where community-based organizations or other government departments are working in the community and find out what capacity and resources these organizations have that could benefit investment activities. This step begins the process of establishing contacts and forming alliances with community organizations and others working toward community investment. Also, any pooling of resources can facilitate the process. National community development organizations, and their intermediaries such as the Enterprise Foundation, the Neighborhood Reinvestment Corporation, and the Local Initiatives Support Corporation are good resources. See Chapter Five for detailed descriptions of these programs.

Collect and Compile Data

A complete list of the data to be compiled for a community credit needs assessment, the first step in this process, can be found on page 33.

Demographics

In terms of demographic indicators, develop a composite picture of the people of your community. Define this information by neighborhood where appropriate. Start by collecting the following data:

- **Population.** Total population, broken down by race, ethnicity, gender, and age.
- **Income and Household Size.** By determining the income and household characteristics, it is possible to anticipate the types of housing needed and the range of costs affordable to the population. Double-income families, single-parent head of households, college students, empty-nesters, fixed-income elderly, public assistance recipients, and single-person households have different needs and resources. In addition, projections of these figures can serve as a basis for estimating future needs.

Data Needed for a Community Credit Needs Assessment

Demographics

Population by race and ethnicity
Age
Income
Per capita income
Percent of population with median income
Percent of population with moderate income
Percent of population with low income
Poverty level

Housing Stock

Number of housing units
Type of housing units
Housing conditions
Housing costs
Housing stock age

Economic Conditions

Total labor force
Unemployment rate
Number of businesses
Number of small businesses
Number of minority- and women-owned businesses

- **Levels of Education.** The level of education (high school, college, graduate school) attained by adult residents also serves as an indicator of potential economic growth.

Demographic profiles can be gathered through several sources already at your fingertips:

- U.S. and State Census Data;
- Local Neighborhood Profiles (prepared by planning or community development agencies);
- Community-based organizations (they often have constituency profiles);

Housing

Housing in the targeted communities should also be examined. Consider factors such as the following:

- **Housing Stock.** Inventory total units, housing stock types (single-family detached, two-family, three-families, multi-families, condominiums), age, and condition to give an initial picture of the housing character for the community.
- **Housing Occupancy.** Identify the percent owner-occupied, percent renter occupied, absentee landlord units, vacant and abandoned properties, waiting lists for subsidized housing.
- **Housing Costs.** Determine current costs for purchase of houses and condominiums; rental prices for apartments, houses, condominiums.
- **Special Issues.** Identify special issues affecting local housing stock such as lead paint and asbestos siding and pipe wrapping. Identify special housing needs including transitional housing, veterans, physically challenged, single parent families, and homeless families and adults.
- **Community Revitalization Plans.** Identify planned or current efforts to improve housing conditions, housing availability, community stabilization.

- **Community Development Organizations.** Identify local actors in development or preservation of affordable housing. Assess their track records and identify future projects and plans.

Data for all of these categories is available through several sources (these are also sources of demographic information):

- Comprehensive Housing Affordability Strategy (CHAS)
- City Planning Reports
- U.S. or State Census Data
- State and Local Community Development Agencies
- Existing Housing Studies (check with community organizations and local colleges/universities for their research)
- Community Development Corporations, other community-based development organizations
- United Way research

Extensive data on housing makes it easier to assess the type of financing — rehabilitation, new construction, mortgages — needed for the community.

Economic Conditions

The economic conditions of low- and moderate-income communities must also be considered. Generally, these communities are depleted of large employers as well as stable small businesses. Identify the following economic development indicators:

- **Local Enterprises.** Identify the types of enterprises (services, professional, technical, retail), their size in terms of receipts and employees, age of business, condition of their properties.
- **Profile of Business Owners.** Determine the number and percentages of women and minority business owners, level of management experience.

■ **Factors Inhibiting Their Growth.** Identify inhibiting factors such as insufficient capital, cash flow, management experience, location, level of technical assistance available.

■ **Major Employers.** Identify the industries and companies that employ significant numbers of local residents. Look at employment trends (seasonal, industry upturns or downturns), skills required (labor, technical, management), and employee services (day care, housing, skills training).

■ **Economic Development Strategies.** Identify local government plans and strategies for assisting and promoting existing businesses and encouraging new businesses and industries.

These agencies generate and collect useful data on business and employment conditions on the local level:

■ State Departments of Labor and Commerce;
■ Chambers of Commerce;
■ Small Business Census Data;
■ Small Business Development Centers affiliated with local colleges;
■ Local Offices of Commerce and Economic Development;
■ Local Trade Organizations;
■ Surveys of Local Businesses.

Analyzing the Financial Market

Analyzing the inventory of current capital resources and the markets they serve is an important component of a comprehensive needs assessment. It will help identify gaps among capital providers and opportunities for expanding existing resources or creating new ones. A financial market analysis should begin with the following steps.

Identify Capital Sources

The existing and potential sources of capital for affordable housing development and rehabilitation, small and minority business development, and community-based organizations may include:

- **Federal Programs.** U.S. Small Business Administration programs, Community Development Block Grant funds.
- **State Programs.** State development departments, state housing finance agency, state economic development fund, enterprise zones, bond programs.
- **Local Government Programs.** Local housing and economic development programs.
- **Quasi-Public Programs.** Development finance corporations, equity funds, revolving loan funds, and loan consortia.
- **Private Programs.** Loan consortia, individual bank programs, bank CDCs, community foundations, national development programs (i.e., Local Initiatives Support Corporation, Enterprise Foundation, Neighborhood Housing Services).

Evaluate Local Lending Institutions

Contact the Community Reinvestment Officer, local branch manager, or Chief Executive Officer of local lending institutions, including regional bank branches, to request copies of the CRA Statement and CRA rating/evaluation. Request the Home Mortgage Disclosure Act (HMDA) Statement that discloses information on loan patterns. Also request information on the location of local branches and automated teller machines, banking hours, and any special programs the bank participates in or administers. More details on the evaluation process are explained in Chapter Three.

Request Application Notices from the Regulatory Agencies

Ask to be placed on the mailing lists of the four regulatory agencies (Federal Reserve Bank Board, Office of Thrift Supervision, Federal Deposit Insurance Corporation, and the Office of the Comptroller of the Currency) to receive notice of applications submitted by financial institutions. Applications must be filed for branch closings, mergers, and acquisitions. This will keep you informed of national and local events in the banking environment that may affect the target community or that may be used as a tool to leverage bank capital.

Review Business and Financial Publications

Financial publications have current information regarding the status of the financial industry. Good examples of specific information sources to become aware of and review are *The Wall Street Journal* and *American Banker*. Also review regional business publications which contain information on current trends and the economic climate.

Evaluate Potential Impact of Capital Sources

Once you have identified available capital sources, evaluate their availability and impact on the city's low- and moderate-income communities.

- Which programs are most useful in the targeted communities? What makes them so?
- Which financial institutions have the strongest presence in these communities? Which have the weakest presence? Why?
- What are the relative costs to the community?
- What types of financing are most needed?
- What are the barriers to access by low- and moderate-income areas?
- Which city resources would best leverage additional private capital and technical/professional resources?

Answers to these questions will reveal gaps in financing for community and economic development in your low- and moderate-income areas. Draw up statements of financing needs to go with the data and needs analysis of community issues. These narrative statements should tie in the information gathered through surveys, interviews, and data sources.

Document the Results

Write a narrative to accompany the data you have gathered. Compile and analyze the information about the people, local housing, and economic development individually and collectively, asking the following questions:

- What is the current state of housing? What has been the trend and what are future projections?
- What are the housing gaps for the resident population?
- What are the local housing development priorities and what strategies exist for their implementation?
- What housing development projects have been completed? How? Why? By Whom?
- What are the major industries? What are the conditions of women- and minority-owned businesses?
- What is the commercial history of the community? What are projected changes?
- Where are service companies located? Are they convenient to all neighborhoods (including lower-income and minority neighborhoods)?
- What problems are impeding further development? Examine failures.
- What mechanisms exist for public and private cooperation and what financing techniques are available?
- Who are the key private and public participants in the development process and what techniques work locally to bring about cooperation?

Answers to these and related questions will reveal gaps in housing and services and future development plans for your low-

and moderate-income areas. Finally, prepare narrative needs statements that can be supported by your findings.

The City's Community Investment Strategy: Setting Precise and Measurable Goals

The information that emerges from the needs assessment process is a tool that can help you address issues already identified in your community. Now that you have identified the credit needs and analyzed the capital market and financing gaps in your city's low- and moderate-income communities and identified sources of capital available from intermediaries, you can begin to outline development goals and the financing needed to accomplish them.

Public funds for community and economic development can leverage substantial private investment. The use of public funds can generate private financing equivalent to two to four times the public investment. This leverage factor tremendously increases the access to, as well as the affordability of, financing by using more flexible underwriting criteria, reducing interest rates, providing gap financing, lowering closing costs, and providing debt subordination. While public funds are waning, they are still highly attractive to financial institutions because they reduce and spread the risk of default. Moreover, the combination of public and private financing is the most viable means of achieving affordability for low- and moderate-income residents. Remember these points when beginning the process of goal-setting:

■ **Explore all financing options.** Using the needs and resources (private financial, local development capacity, tax-exempt financing, and government programs) that have been identified, develop a list of programs and products that would enable the city to achieve its goals. Re-evaluate the city's current community and economic development plans. Are they

Transit to: I-UNIVLIB
Item ID: 30000036926651
Call number: KF1035 .M39 1991
Title: Local officials guide to the
Reinvestme
Current time: 12/02/2008,7:
Transit date: 12/2/2008,8:36
Transit library: NORTHWEST

thorough enough? Do they take financial institutions into account? How can local lenders get involved? Cities should integrate private resources in the public agenda/plan both in terms of identifying needs and structuring and delivering programs and resources.

■ **Keep your expectations realistic.** A strategic community investment plan that lenders regard as totally unachievable probably will not be well-received. You might determine investment requests based on current housing and small business financing needs and development projections. Establish smaller and short-term initiatives that are followed by long-term or larger projects.

■ **Think also about a potential delivery system.** In planning the implementation of the eventual community investment proposal consider the capacity of existing entities and potential new vehicles (such as loan consortia or bank community development corporations). What agencies and organizations (government, non-profit, private) presently do related tasks? Could their functions be consolidated or expanded?

■ **Determine a time line that is attainable.** An overly aggressive time line is not only unrealistic, but it may alarm the financial institutions. An open-ended process may, however, lose momentum.

Communicating Needs—Building a Consensus

Development of a comprehensive Community Investment Plan requires the commitment and cooperation of the city, local financial institutions, and community organizations. This is the most complex phase in the process and the most difficult to anticipate. Personalities among the leadership in each sector weigh heavily in the process and outcome. Establishing the dialogue could take several forms.

■ Local lenders may approach the city and community organizations individually during the process of ascertaining community credit needs.

■ Community organizations may confront lenders on their lending practices and request certain remedies.

■ The city may approach the lenders and community leaders to develop a rational, comprehensive Community Investment Plan that achieves the goals and objectives of all the interested parties.

How should the city approach its local lenders? There are two basic ways, with variations on each theme.

Collectively

For a comprehensive effort, the elected local official could invite all financial institutions that serve the area to a meeting or forum to discuss the credit needs of the community. Depending on the relationships and track records of the institutions, the meeting could be scheduled as the local government embarks on its needs assessment (by including lender participation in the process – they could use it for their CRA requirements) or after the assessment has been completed (to provide reactions to the finished product).

There are several incentives for lenders to participate, and they should be communicated early and often. These incentives include:

■ Provides documentation for CRA files
■ Facilitates needs assessment process
■ Educates community about bank
■ Familiarizes bank officers with community issues
■ Demonstrates commitment to the community
■ Reduces risk through collective efforts
■ Identifies untapped markets
■ Initiates public/private partnerships

Individually

Another method is to approach banks on an individual basis. Often the tendency is to seek participation from the lenders who have been most active with city and community programs. Those who are not as active, however, should also be approached; they may be seeking more community investment activity.

The most important effect of establishing dialogue is the political tone it creates. While a confrontational tone may result in defensive and acrimonious dialogue, interests that are too cordial may not be creative or resourceful enough to resolve complex issues. A certain amount of tension can be a healthy part of the process.

Cultivating leadership in each sector is critical to the success of this process. The importance of a sense of ownership or "buy-in" on the part of lenders cannot be overstated, and it should be communicated early and often. The financial institutions need to have a vested interest in the process and realize the benefits of participation and the risks of withdrawing. Community leaders must be confident in their mission and be willing to exert CRA and media pressure when necessary to keep the process moving. The city must also provide strong and consistent leadership, prodding the process and assuring government cooperation. The city may choose to play the role of consensus-builder among the parties (lenders and community organizations).

Input from the various sectors can ensure realistic and feasible programs and services. This consensus-building process also calls for the greatest amount of time, negotiation, and communication among the groups.

Development of a Community Investment Plan

As previously mentioned, the development of a community investment plan is a critical element to increasing lender participation in low- and moderate-income communities. Establishing the issues and bringing consensus from all interested parties is necessary to accomplish the end goal of increasing investment and improving your low- and moderate-income areas. The following steps describe the development process of a community investment strategy and plan.

1. Establish Task Forces

Once the need for discussion is established with local financial institutions, the groups may determine that task forces are appropriate mechanisms for examining the issues and developing solutions. The most successful programs emerge from groups that offer different perspectives: lenders, city officials, community development organizations, community-based organizations, small business representatives. Task forces may be established to identify and describe credit needs, such as affordable housing development, mortgage lending, economic development, and minority and small businesses. An open but structured process will keep the focus on the agreed-upon issues and allow all interested parties to participate. Delegate responsibility to various members to keep them involved and vested in the process.

One issue to consider is who should chair the task forces. Local lenders tend to become committed and remain active when they are responsible for the direction and progress of the groups. Lenders will also seek to expedite the process because they have the responsibilities of their banks to attend to. City officials may also choose to chair the task forces, but the chairpersons should have sufficient status to maintain interest and commitment.

2. Draw on the City's Community Investment Strategy and Proposal

The city should use the community investment plan based on its community credit needs assessment and financial market analysis. Depending on local dynamics, the city may unveil specific elements of the plan as the process unfolds. Alternatively, presentation of the full plan may serve as the negotiation paper for the process.

Community leaders may have developed their own proposals for discussion as well. The city should work closely with local nonprofit community developers, community action agencies, minority leaders, and church and social service representatives to incorporate their issues and needs in the resulting Community Investment Plan. Dialogue with these individuals and organizations can begin as you develop the community credit needs assessment. Many of their issues and concerns will be uncovered as you go through that process.

3. Establish Time Lines

Incremental deadlines will keep the process moving. Individuals will become involved as they see their issues addressed. Recognize progress as it occurs to keep morale positive.

4. Develop an Accepted Community Investment Plan.

Integrate the feedback through the task force discussion process to develop a comprehensive Community Investment Plan. Use commitments and expertise from all participants to ensure a well-rounded and viable program. Consider housing development, homeownership, rental housing, small and minority business development, and basic bank services in your plan.

5. Market the Process and Programs. Once agreement and consensus have been reached and a community investment plan has been devised, it is important to publicize the program. Distribute information on the goals and objectives of the process and participants. Include the names of the individuals and organizations involved and their individual contributions. Widespread marketing of community investment programs not only informs the community of new opportunities and programs that will benefit them, but it attracts other resources. Increased knowledge of your community investment plan can only improve your chances for success.

By understanding the structural and capital needs of the low- and moderate-income communities, the resources and limitations of the nonprofit community-based organizations, and

Sample Outline for Community Investment Plan

I. Statement of Need

Before a plan can be identified, a statement of need outlining the issues in your community must be developed. Use the information gathered from the Community Credit Needs Assessment.

A. Demographic Profile

Within the general profile, identify special populations within your community (i.e., elderly, non-English speaking groups, single-parents).

B. Housing
1. Development/Rehabilitation
2. Mortgages for Homeownership
3. Rental Needs

C. Economic Development
1. Small and Minority-owned Businesses
2. Local Industries' Needs
3. Job/Skills Training

D. Basic Financial Services in the Community
1. Checking/Savings Accounts
2. Consumer Education
3. Access to Services

II. Current Responses

Summarize the resources, programs, products, and services offered to meet the needs of the community. Again, most of this information can be gathered from information in the Community Credit Needs Assessment and city reports.

A. By the City
B. By the Private Sector
C. By the Nonprofit Sector

III. Community Investment Goals and Responses

The information of the first two sections frames the discussion and detail for the rest of the Community Investment Plan. With the needs and current responses clearly identified, the recommendations of the plan are placed in a context which is consistent for all participants. This is the heart of the Community Investment Plan, as it describes new approaches to address the issues and reach the goals of the community. The format of this section will vary according to the responses (that is, products and delivery vehicles) you develop to address the issues. In general, though, it is recommended that the style be consistent with the previous sections of the plan.

A. Housing Development
Goals and Responses
B. Mortgage Products
Goals and Responses
C. Economic Development
Goals and Responses
D. Basic Financial Services
Goals and Responses

the involvement of the financial institutions, the city can work through a rational process to maximize the progress in its communities.

Designing the City's Community Investment Plan

A Community Investment Plan can take many forms. Examples to consider include those from the cities of West Hollywood, California; Chicago, Illinois; and others. The box on page 46 presents an outline you can use to develop a Community Investment Plan for your city.

The purposes for the Community Investment Plan should be defined. The plan can serve as a strategic plan or guide for addressing community needs. It can be a dynamic, working document until all programmatic responses are in place. Sections of the plan may be extracted for marketing the plan to potential investors, community organizations, and residents.

The heart of the Community Investment Plan is the section on Community Investment Goals and Responses, as that section describes new approaches to address the issues and reach the goals of the community. The plan may include a variety of programmatic responses. Programs may include certain products (construction financing, soft second mortgages, permanent financing, small business lending, technical assistance) and delivery vehicles (loan consortia, micro-enterprise loan pools, technical assistance centers).

When you're developing this plan, consider the existing technical and financial resources and plans for community and economic development. Look for ways to leverage the commitments of all parties to generate the greatest impact on the community.

Evaluating the CRA Performance of Local Banks

CRA gives you the opportunity to increase local bank involvement in your city's community and economic development plans. Recent emphasis and guidelines from the regulators' CRA policy statement and the public disclosure of CRA ratings, have made financial institutions more aware of their community reinvestment responsibilities than ever before. The financial institutions are looking for ways to comply with CRA at minimal expense.

When discussing the CRA with your local financial institutions, it is important to know how and what they are doing in the communities they serve in your city. Public officials and administrators have several useful tools at their disposal that increase their ability to evaluate financial institutions from a standpoint of community reinvestment. You can help banks meet local banking needs by suggesting programs. Be creative.

CRA Ratings by Federal Regulators

One of the most useful tools available to local public officials is the federal regulators' ratings of financial institutions' compliance with CRA. Reviewing a bank's rating (outstanding, satisfactory, needs to improve, or substantial noncompliance) can give you a preliminary sense of how the financial institution is performing in regard to CRA. Examiners now also include written evaluations on each of the assessment factors that indicate the issues and programs they uncovered and their evaluation of bank responses.

Although the new public ratings are useful, there are three things to be careful about when you use this information. First, ratings are available only for financial institutions that have been examined since July 1990. Public CRA ratings or evaluations may not be immediately available for all banks in a community. As a result, their use may be extremely limited initially, but it will increase over time as more examinations are completed. Second, the regulators themselves have been criticized for being too lenient in examining and rating financial institutions for CRA compliance. Third, city officials should keep in mind that a bank's CRA ratings and evaluation provide only a snapshot in time. A bank's CRA performance could change after the evaluation is released. Analyze CRA ratings in conjunction with other information and your own analysis of that information. For these reasons, maintaining a continuing dialogue with local banks will continue to be the best method for city officials to use.

City government can be proactive in this process by providing public comment on the institution's involvement in its community. Letters addressing the bank's record before an examination and the examiner's evaluation/rating should note that the correspondence is to be placed in the bank's CRA Public Comment File. It is also strongly suggested to provide a copy of any comment letters to the bank's supervisory agency.

Bank CRA Statements

Another useful tool for evaluating a financial institution is the Bank CRA Statement. CRA statements are required by federal regulators, and they must be provided by all financial institutions and made available to the general public. Bank CRA Statements are a significant leveraging factor for lenders and cities. That is, the Bank CRA Statement would make a smart bank *want* a city's help. A bank's CRA statement must include basic information on the geographic boundaries of its community; the location, services, and hours of its branches; the types of credit products it offers; and the CRA Notice, which informs the public of CRA requirements.

Although the above information is all that is formally required, federal regulators strongly encourage financial institutions to provide additional information in their CRA statements. As outlined in the Joint Policy Statement, federal regulators recommend banks include information in three general areas:

- descriptions of their efforts to determine community credit needs;
- how their efforts help meet community credit needs; and
- periodic reports on their efforts to meet community credit needs.

Financial institutions may include detailed descriptions of the methods they use to ascertain community credit needs. In addition to ascertaining needs, it is in the best interest of banks to document — for both regulators and the public — exactly how they determined their communities' credit needs. Descriptions of the methods used (such as data collection, meetings with public officials, work with community-based organizations) as well as the information obtained should be included in an institution's expanded CRA statement. Information on population, income, housing stock, housing conditions, housing costs, the types and number of businesses, and the efforts of community-based development organizations is all pertinent to determining the credit needs of a community.

Information on how bank efforts help meet community needs should include details on the institution's participation with government loan programs; relationships with community-based organizations involved in development; loans to development projects sponsored by community-based organizations; and participation in public/private partnerships targeting community development.

In reporting their efforts to meet community credit needs, financial institutions may include in their CRA statements quarterly reports that document their contacts (through phone calls, meetings, conferences, seminars, or other means) with community-based organizations and public agencies; the types, amounts, and locations of loans made in low- and moderate-income neighborhoods; and staff, management, and board member participation in civic and community-based organizations. This information will demonstrate an institution's commitment to its community and its determination to proactively attain its market share of customers and loans in low- and moderate-income areas.

Bank Responses to Community Needs

Examine the steps the financial institution took to meet these needs. For example, the regulatory agencies suggests several activities for bank involvement. Use the activities listed below as a reference checklist when you evaluate lender activity in your city. Remember, though, that this list is only a starting point; you should develop your own list.

Increase availability of existing products and services.

- Implement policies, including the use of more flexible lending criteria, consistent with safe and sound practices.
- Participation in various government-insured lending programs and other types of lending programs, such as high loan-to-value ratio conventional mortgage loans with private mortgage insurance to help meet identified credit needs.
- Develop and advertise loan programs and other bank services to benefit low- and moderate-income persons,

such as subsidized mortgage loans or government check cashing and low-cost checking accounts.

Target an advertising and marketing strategy to inform low- and moderate-income groups of available loan and deposit services.

- Identify means to reach these groups (for example, community newspapers, radio, television, community and church organizations, non-English literature).
- Expand officer call programs to include targeted groups in low- and moderate-income neighborhoods including small business owners and real estate agents.

Involvement of high level bank officers.

- Establish a process involving all levels of management in efforts to contact governmental leaders, economic development practitioners, businesses and business associations, and community organizations to discuss the financial services that are needed by the community.
- Develop corporate policy containing provisions for public notice of branch closings, accompanied with an impact analysis of such a closing to the local community, and efforts to minimize any adverse effects.

Bank involvement in community investment programs.

- Participate in and assist local and state housing, economic, and community development programs and projects.
- Establish a bank community development corporation.
- Fund a small business investment corporation or a minority enterprise/small business investment corporation.
- Make lines of credit and other financing available, within prudent lending principles, to nonprofit developers of low-income housing and small business

development, and/or provide a secondary market for nonprofit developer paper.

■ Invest in municipal bonds.

■ Participate in the Federal Home Loan Bank's Community Investment Fund and Affordable Housing programs when applicable.

■ Establish a pilot or special lending program for low- and moderate-income neighborhoods.

Minimal efforts in any of these areas demonstrate extremely weak bank policies and programs for serving the community.

How To Use HMDA

The demographic information on mortgage applicants required by the Home Mortgage Disclosure Act gives local officials a useful tool to evaluate the investment levels of all financial institutions in their communities. Background on HMDA can be found in Chapter One. Here are some factors to consider when reviewing HMDA data of local financial institutions:

■ **Geography:** Look for geographic patterns of investment. Are loans concentrated in or absent from certain areas or neighborhoods? Where are loan applications coming from?

■ **Income:** Identify income levels of loan applicants in relation to neighborhood median income.

■ **Race and gender:** Identify the race and gender of applicants, both those approved and declined. Compare with relative incomes and location of properties.

These expanded reporting requirements allow a better review of mortgage lending patterns, a useful part of evaluating bank performance in your community.

Review Bank Marketing and Outreach

Analyze marketing efforts, branch locations, bank hours. Consider the following questions:

- Where are bank branches located? ATMs?
- What are the branch hours in each?
- What is the bank presence in low- and moderate-income areas and communities of color?
- Are bank personnel bilingual in multi-cultural neighborhoods?
- Are bank marketing materials understandable to non-English speaking residents?
- What are the outreach efforts to these communities? To small and minority-owned businesses?

If further analysis continues to demonstrate the bank's failure to meet community credit needs, local public officials can seize this opportunity to leverage capital for community reinvestment through CRA dialogue and negotiations.

CRA Roles for City Officials:
Two Case Studies

While some local financial institutions are willing to participate in community development-oriented programs, many others remain reluctant. This creates a need and an opportunity for local officials to step up efforts to use CRA to leverage resources. As part of their efforts to influence banks' community investment decisions, city officials are actively engaging banks in discussions and negotiations to forge practical and viable community reinvestment strategies.

This chapter presents two case studies showing the different roles city government can assume in influencing the development of CRA initiatives. The particular examples — CRA efforts in West Hollywood, California, and Boston, Massachusetts — were chosen because they illustrate how CRA programs and policies devised with input from public officials result in creative ventures with short- and long-term promise for financial institutions and communities. The West Hollywood case shows how a city can employ a rational, strategic approach to using the CRA and facilitate the negotiations and discussions between diverse interests. The Boston case study reveals how, amid debate and contention, a city can act as an advocate for CRA and use other vehicles of negotiation to leverage significant resources for the city.

There are considerable contrasts between the roles the city played in both cases and between the impetus for the initiatives. In Boston, negotiations took place against a backdrop of pressure from the media, which released preliminary Federal Reserve study findings and followed the negotiations closely throughout the year-long process. This added to the urgency to develop the Community Investment Plan, the five-year, multi-bank investment program to meet a host of community credit needs.

By contrast, the West Hollywood Plan did not develop in an atmosphere of close scrutiny or heated controversy from the media or the community. In West Hollywood, much of the credit for the use of CRA to leverage additional capital and bank services from local financial institutions belongs to the informed staff of the city's Department of Community Development. After attending a National League of Cities conference and learning how the CRA can benefit everyone—banks, the city, and the community—the department staff initiated discussions with the local financial institutions and the community in a forum intended to raise issues of concern regarding community reinvestment needs and banks' role in addressing those needs.

Both West Hollywood and Boston emerged from their discussions with the community and banking industry with substantive programs targeted to the needs of the community in several critical areas—affordable housing, small and minority business development, and consumer banking services.

City as Facilitator: Department of Community Development West Hollywood, California

West Hollywood, incorporated in 1984, is a diverse city with a variety of ethnic and racial enclaves. It is home to 37,000 individuals who differ in age, socioeconomic level, and lifestyle preference. As would be expected with such a diverse community, there are a number of concerns and issues affecting the quality of life for the community.

The City of West Hollywood realized that meeting the needs of its residents required greater resources than the city had available. This was especially evident in the city's low- and moderate- income communities and in the growing immigrant and elderly populations, both of which face challenges in housing affordability, special needs housing, small business development, and consumer banking services.

Process

In the fall of 1988, at the urging of the city's Department of Housing and Economic Development, the city held a forum on the Community Reinvestment Act. Among those attending were community representatives, bank officials, and Federal Home Loan Bank of San Francisco officials. At this meeting a number of community concerns were raised by the various groups in attendance.

Before the meeting, the city had done a limited assessment of community credit and bank service needs. What became apparent to city officials was the need to leverage their limited resources with additional resources from the private sector. The CRA provided the most appropriate leveraging tool.

A task force was established to address the community concerns identified at the meeting. The task force included individuals who attended the first meeting, as well as others whow knew about community credit and service needs and were interested in developing a community reinvestment plan. Elected city officials, community housing advocates, chamber of commerce officers, and local senior level bank representatives and CRA officers participated in the process. Many of the bank representatives lived in the community, knew the community's needs, and were interested in ways to direct additional resources to these areas.

Because of the broad nature of the community's concerns, the task force was divided into two working subcommittees. One group focused on problems and solutions related to housing concerns; the other focused on small business economic development and consumer banking services.

With the partnerships firmly established, the task force and subcommittees began to consider strategies for a comprehensive community reinvestment program. As part of the process of designing the Community Reinvestment Plan, the task force set out to identify reinvestment programs and vehicles used successfully in other parts of the state and country. In addition to being replicable, many of these reinvestment strategies are established on a statewide or regional basis in California. Not only did these established programs provide models for the city, but they provided additional resources to the city, community, and local financial institutions.

West Hollywood staff characterize the negotiations that took place between the city, community advocates, and financial institutions as educational sessions, not adversarial debates. Community and city representatives learned of banks' limitations and why certain proposals were not feasible for banks. Banks learned of existing services and programs aimed at responding to community needs in which they could participate. The banking community also found there were changes they could make in policies and procedures that would provide greater access to capital and services for the community, such as relaxed underwriting criteria and bilingual tellers.

The completed draft reinvestment plan was presented to the local banking community for further comment. After the banking community's concerns had been addressed and incorporated in the overall document, it was sent to the city council for adoption as the official Community Reinvestment Plan of West Hollywood.

Results

The Community Reinvestment Plan was adopted by the City in June 1989, less than a year after the initial meeting. The plan is a far-reaching reinvestment program intended to be a resource for financial institutions in their community reinvestment efforts. It offers short- and long-term strategies for addressing specific issues in the areas of housing, small business development, and bank services and products.

The focus of the plan is a compilation of short- and long-term investment strategies. The strategies provide a menu from which local banks and savings and loans can select ways to fulfill CRA requirements and meet the credit and bank service needs of the community.

Small Business Development

Accessing capital and support for small business growth and development is one of the greatest economic development challenges facing any city. Financing for startup and small businesses is usually obtained from family or friends, personal savings, or personal loans from financial institutions. Banks are reluctant to make commercial loans for startup and small businesses because the loan amounts are usually small and the business owners are sometimes not familiar with business loan procedures. Additionally, the time required by banks to review such loans is as much or more than the time required for larger loan requests, which are more profitable.

In West Hollywood, small business owners and would-be business owners faced these obstacles and more. The West Hollywood community includes a large population of Russian immigrants who lack business or managerial skills and are unfamiliar with lending practices.

The city has enacted several strategies to maintain the momentum gained during the development of the plan. A city-sponsored women's self-employment workshop helps women develop business plans and gain the technical skills needed to start businesses. Women who complete the twelve-week program are eligible for $2,000 seed grants, donated annually by banks, to begin their operations.

A micro-loan program, established with a portion of the city's Community Development Block Grant (CDBG), is leveraged against bank financing for a total of $150,000 available for businesses in need of financing between $1,000 and $25,000. The banks offer a lower interest rate on these funds.

Banks also relaxed their requirements for collateral and underwriting criteria for small businesses that were leveraged with start-up phase of operation.

Affordable Housing

Federal cutbacks in housing subsidies and a lack of private sector funding have all significantly affected the city's ability to introduce affordable housing programs. As part of its long-term strategy, the city identified a number of established state- and countywide programs that could help financial institutions, the city, and local housing developers begin to address this need. Among the vehicles identified were several statewide loan consortia established by banks specifically for affordable housing lending. These consortia and loan pools allow banks to contribute both their capital and technical expertise to affordable housing developers and projects. The city also intends to encourage financial institutions to take advantage of other sources such as the secondary mortgage market programs, which provide equity and tax credits for investments in low- and moderate-income housing projects.

In addition to the need for traditional low- and moderate-income housing, West Hollywood has many elderly and gay residents who often have special housing needs. The city's plan identifies local and state resources that address the special housing needs of these populations and informs local banks about how they can participate in these types of projects.

The city is also concentrating on strategies for adapting and rehabilitating properties for seismic safety.

Consumer Banking Services

Because the CRA focuses on credit issues, discussions of CRA obligations and reinvestment strategies tend to focus on issues of lending for housing and economic development. As a result, the need for financial institutions to provide basic consumer banking services for their community is often lost in the discussion. These services include accessible and available bank facilities and bank products appropriate to the community's immediate and future needs.

West Hollywood residents — specifically fixed-income elderly and low-income residents — do not have adequate access to consumer bank services such as life-line checking, government check cashing programs, and low- or no-fee deposit accounts. Along with these services, consumers need education about the banking industry and how to access services that meet their needs. Other needed services include hiring and training of bank staff, especially those working directly with customers in need of bilingual services, convenient bank hours, and additional bank branches.

In response to the basic consumer needs of the community, the city identified several areas where its assistance enhances service and educational provisions from the banking community. The immediate strategies the city has enacted include assembling an information and guide book on various bank products and services offered by local financial institutions. To further the educational process and keep banks apprised of the community's banking needs, the city and banks sponsor workshops and seminars to ascertain the community's banking needs and devise additional strategies to meet these needs.

The city will continue to encourage the area's financial institutions to seek reinvestment opportunities by urging them to adopt special bank services such as life-line checking for senior citizens and low-income residents.

For more information: Rhonda Sherman, City of West Hollywood, Housing and Economic Development Division, 8611

Santa Monica Boulevard, West Hollywood, CA 90069-4109; (213) 854-7475.

City as Advocate: City of Boston, Massachusetts

In 1989, to the surprise of many and the dismay of others, redlining once again emerged as a major issue in Boston. During the 1970s, bankers and community organizations clashed over the alleged redlining in Boston's minority and low-income communities. Twenty years later, these same banks and community groups – plus a new group of players, local government officials – were again embroiled in lengthy discussions and negotiations around the issue of community reinvestment for Boston's neighborhoods.

Long before discussions between these various groups began, the City of Boston had been working successfully with community-based development organizations to construct and rehabilitate affordable housing and make capital improvements in neighborhoods. Much of the funding for these activities was derived from a linkage program that directed funds from downtown developments to the city's affordable housing programs.

Despite the city's efforts to carry out community investment activities, many development projects still required private lender participation for mortgages and construction financing. The city found that local banks invested in local development projects, but only on a highly selective basis, and that there was a lack of clearly-defined criteria, especially for affordable housing development. Many banks did not fully understand the nature of affordable housing lending and viewed it as a risky proposition. Because each project is unique, financing must be tailored specifically to the project, a time-consuming undertaking for banks and perceivably not as profitable as larger construction deals. Those banks familiar with affordable housing projects were mainly aware of local public-private housing partnership efforts such as the Boston Housing Partnership, which packages funding and financing for the construction and rehabilitation of affordable housing units by community development corporations.

Process

To determine if these perceptions were accurate, the Boston Redevelopment Authority, the city's planning agency, proposed a study to analyze the mortgage lending patterns of banks in Boston's neighborhoods. Shortly after this study was proposed, preliminary findings from a similar study by the Federal Reserve Bank of Boston were leaked to the press. The early findings of the Federal Reserve study uncovered substantial disparities in mortgage lending patterns based on race and geography. Clearly, the city's perceptions were borne out by the preliminary analyses.

Responding to the implications of these findings, the city and community activists demanded that local financial institutions address the problems of redlining and mortgage lending disparities. The banking industry, while not acknowledging the practice of redlining, did concede that there were lending disparities between black and white communities. This disparity, they insisted, existed because of differences in demand for mortgages, not because of discriminatory practices on the part of the banks. However, the Massachusetts Bankers Association (MBA) and the Federal Reserve Bank of Boston, in response to the growing controversy, initiated a series of public forums to identify other community banking and credit needs.

The city and the Community Investment Coalition (CIC), an alliance of several community-based organizations, continued to apply pressure to the banking industry to address the issues that had emerged. The city also continued to urge the banking industry to work with existing city programs and community-based organizations to develop workable solutions. Both the city and the CIC designed detailed reinvestment strategies to be considered by the banks. As a result of the public forums, the MBA formed four task forces of bankers, city and state officials, and community representatives. These task forces were to identify alternatives and make recommendations to meet the communities needs articulated at the forums. The lengthy and sometimes intense discussions that began with the task forces would eventually lead to a comprehensive program of community investment.

In an effort to further negotiations with banks, the city passed a "linked deposit" ordinance that allows the city to regularly examine banks' lending records in the areas of housing, small business, and participation in city-sponsored housing and neighborhood development programs. Additionally, the city would examine banks' records for hiring minority personnel, branch location, hours of operation, and other services that meet the needs of low- and moderate-income customers. The city will only deposit public funds with banks having commendable records regarding community and neighborhood reinvestment and services.

Meanwhile, the final versions of the Federal Reserve Bank of Boston and city reports, released in August and December of 1989 respectively, put additional pressure on the task forces to arrive at a strategy for bank reinvestment. Both reports documented significant disinvestment on the part of banks in black and low-income neighborhoods that directly contributed to their decline.

Amid the reports and alternative reinvestment plans and policies, negotiations continued between the various parties. In January 1990, the statewide, five-year MBA $400 million Community Investment Program was announced.

Results

As a result of the year-long discussions between the community representatives, the bankers, and city and state government officials, three new corporations were created to address community credit needs.

Consumer Education

The Massachusetts Community and Banking Council (MCBC) was created to provide education both to communities and banks and to act as an advisory council to member banks. The Council promotes community investment and new bank programs, such as low- or no-fee checking and government check cashing programs, and helps assess community credit needs. MCBC also monitors the overall implementation of the MBA Community Investment Program.

One of the first tangible outcomes of the Community Investment Program occurred in the spring of 1990, when the city and the newly created MCBC cosponsored a mortgage fair targeting first-time home buyers in Boston's Roxbury neighborhood. The 1,200 potential home buyers who attended the event gathered information and began relationships with fourteen banks and seventeen other organizations, including local developers, financial/credit counselors, and housing advocates. MCBC also inaugurated a voluntary government check cashing program with 200 participating banks and their 1,800 branches across the state.

Affordable Housing

The Massachusetts Housing Investment Corporation (MHIC) was designed as a $100 million loan consortium to finance the purchase, rehabilitation, and construction of affordable housing projects. It also has a $100 million equity fund to coordinate investments by banks and other corporations in federal low-income housing tax credit projects.

Another element of the Community Investment Program designed to meet first-time home buyers' mortgage needs is a $100 million program with Federal National Mortgage Association (Fannie Mae), General Electric Mortgage Insurance Corporation, and several statewide banks. Qualifying first-time home buyer applicants can purchase homes in targeted communities with much more flexible underwriting criteria. A number of banks also created their own first-time home buyer programs, and a "soft second" mortgage program was created to help home buyers with down payments.

Minority Business Development

The Massachusetts Minority Enterprise Investment Corporation (MMEIC) was created to increase the access to debt and equity capital for businesses owned by minority or disadvantaged owners. Capitalized with $5 million, MMEIC is a for-profit, multi-bank Community Development Corporation (CDC) with the goal of mainstreaming minority-owned businesses into traditional bank relationships. MMEIC will provide both debt and equity capital for businesses in need of capital between $2,500 and $250,000. The MMEIC also has a wholly owned, SBA-licensed Minority Enterprise Small Business Investment Corporation (MESBIC) that provides equity for sizable investments.

For more information:

Massachusetts Community and Banking Council, Joseph Feaster, Executive Director, 100 Franklin Street, Mezzanine Level, Boston, Massachusetts 02101; (617) 423-4449.

Massachusetts Housing Investment Corporation, Joseph Flatley, President, 100 Franklin Street, Mezzanine Level, Boston, Massachusetts 02110; (617) 338-6886.

Massachusetts Minority Enterprise Investment Corporation, Thomas Schumpert, President, 100 Franklin Street, Mezzanine Level, Boston, Massachusetts 02110; (617) 338-0425.

Minority Enterprise Small Business Investment Corporation, Milton Benjamin, President, Community Development Finance Corporation, Ten Post Office Square, Suite 1090, Boston, Massachusetts 02109; (617) 482-9141.

CHAPTER FIVE

Implementing Programs and Policies:
Model Programs and Vehicles

This chapter summarizes several case studies and model programs to show how cities and states that have undertaken a CRA planning process can use financial and non-financial tools to increase community and economic revitalization. These case studies and model programs were chosen because they represent a wide variety of potential responses and outcomes that can be used by the local government officials and financial institutions individually and in partnership efforts. Partnerships can be instrumental in developing assistance programs that meet the various financing needs of most communities, especially low- and moderate-income communities. Cities, states, and financial institutions can participate in capital investment pools and use public funds to effectively stimulate economic growth and development.

Although, each city, state, or private institution is unique in its approach to community economic development, its participation demonstrates the importance of institutional support in stimulating revitalization. The model programs and vehicles are divided into four sections—Local Public Programs, Public-Private Programs, Private Programs, and Intermediary Programs.

Types of Programs and Vehicles: A Glossary

Bank Community Development Corporation (Bank CDC)

A bank sponsored subsidiary corporation created to facilitate community economic development and investment initiatives in areas such as housing, small business, industrial, and other needs in low- and moderate-income communities.

Bank Lending Unit

A specialized bank unit designed to initiate community reinvestment loans for housing and economic development in low- and moderate-income communities.

Housing Trust Fund

Public sector pool of capital, generally funded by a state or local revenue stream, used to provide low- and moderate-income housing.

Housing Partnership

Collaborative ventures by public and private organizations for the production and maintenance of housing stock affordable to low- and moderate-income households.

Loan Consortium

A source of loan capital from private financial institutions for economic growth and the development and rehabilitation of housing units affordable to low- and moderate-income people.

Local Public Housing and Community Development Programs

Public programs initiated by the local public sector specifically designed to leverage private sector capital.

Publicly Sponsored Development Corporations

These are quasi-public corporations, usually not for profit, that are sponsored by local or state government but have private investment or members.

National Intermediary Programs

National organizations created to improve low- and moderate-income communities through programs and services. Programs target housing, economic development, and overall community revitalization.

Local Public Programs

Local public programs are typically administered by city housing and economic development departments or authorities to support the economic growth and development of neighborhood commercial businesses, industries, and community-based development organizations. The programs assist in efforts to create and maintain jobs and industries. Support for these organizations is provided through loans, grants, and technical assistance. The programs promote public sector leadership in economic and community development. The local programs described in this chapter represent various aspects of local public programs designed to meet financial and technical assistance needs.

This section presents four public programs from different parts of the country: the Baltimore County Economic Development Commission, the Chicago Department of Housing, the Dade County Stamp Surtax Trust Fund, and the Kenosha Uptown Business Improvement District.

Baltimore County Economic Development Commission, Baltimore, Maryland

The City and County of Baltimore are both extremely diverse geographic regions in terms of population, housing conditions, and economic conditions. Although some areas of the city and county have stable economic environments, many neighborhoods have extremely poor community and economic conditions. The Baltimore County Economic Development Commission is designed to strengthen economic development efforts throughout the Baltimore area by developing and providing economic development incentive programs to assist existing businesses and attract new businesses.

Program Activities

The Commission's primary program is the Revitalization Area Fund. This fund provides below-market rate financing in conjunction with Signet Bank/Maryland for businesses in Revitalization Districts and in rural commercial areas. The fund is intended to help communities create permanent full-time jobs for unemployed residents; to retain existing jobs; to provide physical improvements for businesses; to enhance the vitality of local commercial districts; and to stimulate private investment.

Loans are available for a maximum of $40,000 or one-third of the total loan amount, whichever is less. The maximum total loan amount is $120,000. Loans are for a maximum of five years at below market interest rates. There is no fee for the Fund's portion of the loan.

Signet Bank is the only financial institution currently working with the Baltimore County Economic Development Commission (CEDC) Revitalization Area Fund. Signet has committed two dollars to every one dollar loaned by the CEDC Revitalization Fund. Signet has not placed a limit on its commitment to the Revitalization Area Fund and the bank may reduce or waive application fees. After one year, the Revitalization Fund has loaned approximately $1.5 million.

Comments

Despite serving as headquarters for many major corporations, Baltimore continues to have severe economic development problems in particular areas of the city and county. The Revitalization Area Fund has provided a means for the public sector to invest its capital as well as leverage capital from the private sector.

Signet Bank benefits from this arrangement in various ways. CEDC's pre-screening of applicants ensures applicants meet the criteria for the program before their applications are submitted. If the loan is approved, the bank lends its portion of the commitment directly to the applicant. Signet's risk is reduced because CEDC takes a second to Signet on the loan; Signet will be repaid before the CEDC. And along with receiving a good return on investment, the bank is able to meet its obligations under the Community Reinvestment Act (CRA).

The CEDC with funding from the Baltimore County Capital Budget was able to receive a commitment from Signet to match loans made through the Revitalization Area Fund. Loans are matched on a two-to-one basis. Because the CEDC takes a second on the loans, Signet's risk is reduced, making participation more attractive for the bank. As financial institutions must invest in their low- and moderate-income communities, opportunities and incentives like this are attractive to lenders.

Chicago Department of Housing – Chicago, Illinois

Chicago is a city of many neighborhoods and communities – each with its own set of housing problems and conditions. Because the city is fairly old, its housing stock is often in substandard condition. For this reason, the Housing Department has placed an emphasis on helping Chicago residents buy, repair, and build private housing in coordination with private developers and community-based organizations. The Department's programs are designed to leverage private sector capital for housing development and rehabilitation.

Program Activities

The Department's Low-Income Housing Tax Reactivation Program is designed to make better use of the city's existing housing stock. This program encourages the development of affordable housing by working with nonprofit and for-profit developers and assisting them to access tax delinquent properties. The program provides tax delinquent properties through its scavenger sale. In most cases, scavenger sale properties are provided to for-profit and nonprofit developers at the cost of $1 under the condition that the properties be used for affordable housing development. This program is used for multi-family development projects.

The Department also leverages private capital with its Multi-Family Rehabilitation Loan Program. This program provides supplementary financing to help low-income tenants rehabilitate their property. No-interest or low-interest loans are provided to owners of multi-family properties in need of rehabilitation. The loan must be secondary to a market rate loan which is provided by a participating lender. The maximum loan can be for up to $25,000 for a term not to exceed forty years.

The Neighborhood Home Improvement Program provides low-interest, fixed rate loans to owners of one- to four-unit properties. Financing is provided by the city in conjunction with several participating banks and the Illinois Housing Development Authority. This program is available to families with incomes of less than $40,000 in most neighborhoods, and less than $35,000 in selected neighborhoods. They may borrow up to $25,000 for up to fifteen years. The Urban Homestead Program sells vacant and repossessed HUD properties based on the availability of properties and the Department's funds. These properties are sold to low- and moderate-income residents who are then helped to arrange rehabilitation financing with participating banks.

Comments

Programs operated by Chicago's Department of Housing are designed to use a variety of resources. The Housing Department combines its financing along with the City's rich housing stock and private sector capital. By selling tax delinquent properties through its Tax Reactivation Program, the Housing Department increases the number of affordable housing units in the City without expending public funds.

In its programs that do expend public funds, the City augments its resources and reinvestment impact by leveraging private capital from financial institutions. The Housing Department combines its financing — often secondary to private financing — with loans from local financial institutions. There are several incentives for financial institutions to participate. Since it is a combination of public and private financing, the default risk for these loans is shared by the financial institution and the Housing Department. In case of default, the financial institution takes first lien position and thus will be repaid first. These loans are specifically designated for low- and moderate-income individuals and/or low- and moderate-income neighborhoods. As a result, by participating in public programs the financial institution is assured of meeting its CRA requirements (i.e., lending in low- and moderate-income neighborhoods, participating in public programs). In addition, some of the financial institution's staff time is reduced by the necessary pre-qualifying completed by the Housing Department.

Dade County Stamp Surtax Trust Fund — Dade County, Florida

In 1983, state and county legislation created the Dade County Stamp Surtax Trust Fund, which generates income from a real estate transfer tax and dedicates the funds to the development of affordable owner-occupied and rental housing. The surtax is a minimal tax — $.45 on $100 — on the transfer of all commercial and industrial property as well as non-single family dwelling residential property. The fund is overseen by the Dade County Commission and also has an advisory council appointed by the Commission.

Program Activities

The Fund is used to provide financing for new construction by nonprofit and for-profit developers, home improvement loans, and soft second mortgages. Most often the Fund provides second mortgages with thirty-year terms and deferred interest rates. These mortgages, which are combined with conventional, market rate first mortgages, have interest rates of 3 percent to 6 percent and defer interest for the first ten years of the loan. The second mortgage does not begin amortizing until the eleventh year of the loan. In terms of rehabilitation, the Fund provides home improvement loans for a maximum of $20,000 with interest rates of 3 percent to 6 percent. These loans have fairly long terms of up to twenty years. The Fund also provides financing for new construction to nonprofit and for profit developers of affordable multi-family and single-family housing. Since its inception, the fund has generated approximately $50 million with an average annual income of $9 to $12 million. By 1989, this revenue enabled the Fund to assist approximately 2,000 households of which 80 percnet were low-income.

Comments

Community-based organizations are playing an increasingly significant role in the creation of trust funds. They can lobby local, state, and government officials; demonstrate community needs; and assist with the administration of the trust fund. The backing of public officials is essential to the process. Bankers are also essential players in the creation of trust funds. Their input on the feasibility of available financing and the potential role of financial institutions is critical to the overall success and efficacy of trust fund programs. Financial institutions can also benefit from the community reinvestment lending aspect of trust funds.

Institutions that provide financing in conjunction with trust fund loan programs meet their CRA obligations since trust funds specifically target low- and moderate-income individuals and communities. In the programs of the Dade County Trust Fund, local financial institutions provide first mortgages in combination with the Fund's second mortgages. This structure enables financial institutions to share default risk with the public sector and take a first lien position in case of foreclosure. In addition, financial institutions are able to provide financing for affordable housing to low- and moderate-income individuals using market rates and traditional and traditional underwriting guidelines. For its part, the local public sector is able to assist more low- and moderate-income residents by using its capital to leverage additional private sector capital. As a result, the Fund has a greater community reinvestment impact than if it relied solely on public financing.

Kenosha Uptown Business Improvement District — Kenosha, Wisconsin

As a result of a general decline in Uptown Kenosha, a secondary business and commercial district, the Uptown Task Force and the Kenosha NHS conducted a market study to determine steps that could be taken to revitalize the district and keep viable businesses in the area.

The Uptown Kenosha business district is surrounded by two residential neighborhoods. Business district proponents estimated that little or no investment had taken place in the district for the past twenty years. The city also has a growing minority population.

In the Kenosha business district, funds for revitalization activities come from a variety of sources. The city allocated funds for a loan fund targeted for use by the business district. Additionally, area banks have provided rehabilitation financing for district businesses.

Program Activities

The Uptown Business Improvement District (BID) was formed in 1986 as a special assessment district to generate funds for the development, management, maintenance, and promotion of the Uptown commercial district.

The city designated the Uptown area as a targeted community reinvestment district, thus making it eligible for a share of Community Development Block Grant (CDBG) funds. These funds have been used to capitalize a loan pool. The loan pool provides funds to district businesses interested in various business enhancements such as facade improvements, interior rehabilitation, and building reconstruction.

BID members felt one of Kenosha's greatest needs was to improve the image of the business district. Part of this could be accomplished with facade and building improvements. Another approach was to attract a major chain store as an anchor to support the rest of the business district. Not only did the anchor store attract customers to the district, but it provided much needed employment to area residents.

Previously, empty store fronts detracted from the physical appearance of the commercial strip. Once the Uptown District had attracted an anchor store and began physical improvements, promotion and outreach activities became easier. New businesses located in the area on the strength of the increased commercial activity in the district.

The Uptown BID offers no tax incentives to businesses locating within the district. However, the BID does write down the purchase cost of land with CDBG funds if businesses are buying property. Additionally, the loan fund offers funds at below market rate for 10 to 15 percent of any improvement project's total cost. The BID also offers subsidized advertising, marketing, and promotional services to member businesses.

Three local financial institutions have committed funds for rehabilitation for district businesses. Other area financial institutions have made loans in cooperation with the Kenosha Uptown Business Improvement District (BID) where a prior relationship with the applicant existed. There is no actual dollar commitment or dedicated pool of funds from the local financial institutions. Participating financial institutions provide rehabilitation financing to local businesses and, if needed, may supplement their loans with gap financing from the Uptown BID. Applications are taken at both the financial institution and the Uptown BID office and referrals are made between the two entities. Application fees are decided on a case-by-case basis; they may be reduced or waived. The bank, because of its reduced exposure, may offer reduced rate financing. The Uptown BID has a maximum loan amount of $25,000. Committed CDBG funds are leveraged on a 4:1 basis (every $1 in CDBG funds loaned is matched by $4 in private financing).

Comments

The Uptown BID has been able to leverage $200,000 in CDBG funds into $4.1 million in total private reinvestment in four years. Besides administering a loan fund, the BID is beginning to develop property within the district. The Kenosha Redevelopment Authority, with the support and encouragement of the BID, recently purchased property in the BID to prevent private developer speculation. The properties were purchased by BID and two new buildings are currently under construction.

The financial institutions participating in the Kenosha Uptown BID benefit in various ways. The participating financial institutions face a lower exposure to risk on the loans they make. The Uptown BID takes a second position to the bank (that is, the bank receives payment on its portion of the loan before the Uptown BID). In addition, the financial institutions contribute to the overall stability of the communities involved and in turn protect other investments in the area. The banks can meet its obligations under the Community Reinvestment Act (CRA) by making loans in their low- and moderate-income communities.

Public-Private Partnerships

Public-private partnerships use the combined resources of the public and private sectors. The strength of public-private partnerships is their ability to capitalize on these resources and therefore use diversified investment vehicles to finance deals. Public funds can be leveraged with private financing resources to form investment pools for specific markets.

Funds can be allocated for various economic development purposes including low- and moderate-income housing and women- and minority-owned businesses. Funds may also be used for the development or preservation of an area. Partnerships occur primarily between city or county agencies and private organizations such as foundations and financial institutions, although nonprofit development organizations can also play a role in the partnership. Partnerships aim to satisfy needs not currently being met by traditional organizational or financial resources. The cases highlighted represent various aspects of state and local public-private partnerships.

This section describes several public-private partnerships: the Bridgeport Neighborhood Fund, the Development Credit Fund, the Florida Black Business Investment Board, the Massachusetts Housing Investment Corporation, the Massachusetts Minority Enterprise Investment Corporation, the Massachusetts Soft Second Program, and the Michigan Strategic Fund.

Bridgeport Neighborhood Fund — Bridgeport, Connecticut

The Bridgeport Neighborhood Fund (BNF), formed in 1986, is a partnership of bankers, business executives, local government officials, and civic leaders to encourage reinvestment in Bridgeport's neighborhoods. The BNF provides financing for new construction and rehabilitation of affordable multi-family housing and related commercial services.

Program Activities

Structures that qualify for financing under the BNF program include apartment buildings, cooperatives, condominiums, mixed-use buildings, special needs housing, shelters, and transitional housing. Flexible underwriting criteria and affordable financing enables many projects to be developed that would otherwise be hindered in the traditional financing marketplace.

The BNF combines bank funds with state loans, city grants, and other sources to offer loans at below-market interest rates. Typical loans range from $35,000 to $750,000, with a loan-to-value ratio of up to 85 percent (95 percent for nonprofit developers). The loans are set at a five-year fixed rate (one-year adjustable rate for rooming houses) with a maximum thirty-year amortization, twenty-year balloon payment. The interest rate is based on what the project can afford.

The fees incurred for loan applications include a $250 nonrefundable application fee, an appraisal fee, architect/engineering fees, and if the loan is approved, borrowers must pay for BNF's legal fees and a 2 percent commitment fee (1 percent for nonprofit developers).

Comments

Housing partnerships provide flexible means for financial institutions, businesses, and community organizations to work together to improve their local neighborhoods. They serve as a forum for consensus building on community issues and solutions.

Designed to provide "one-stop shopping," housing partnerships typically assemble sources of planning assistance, seed money, equity, construction financing, and long-term financing, as well as provide technical assistance on all phases of housing development and management. The local government facilitates the development of affordable housing through assistance with zoning and codes, and financial subsidies.

Development Credit Fund, Inc., Baltimore, Maryland

Established in 1983, the Development Credit Fund, Inc. (DCF), is a private, not-for-profit statewide organization which administers and approves loans for minority-owned businesses. A study conducted by the Greater Baltimore Committee identified access to greater sources of capital as a major barrier to minority business development. The Greater Baltimore Committee is made up of key businesses, corporations, and lending institutions. These members played a primary role in designing the program. The DCF was created to meet this need and bridge the financing gap for minority and disadvantaged businesses.

Six major banks provided most of the initial funding for the DCF and loaned executives to DCF as it was starting up. The State of Maryland provided a loan guarantee program through the Maryland Small Business Development Finance Authority (MSBDFA). The city of Baltimore also provided a start-up operational grant to DCF.

Program Activities

The DCF is an innovative program that works with banks to ensure they are reinvesting in the communities they serve. The program provides below market rate financing for minority-owned and disadvantaged businesses throughout the state.

Initially, six of Maryland's largest banks provided $7.5 million to DCF at a discounted rate of prime minus 5 percent. DCF, in turn, re-lends the funds at a rate of prime plus one. The rate spread covers the operating costs of DCF. The State, through the MSBDFA, provides a $7.5 million loan guarantee fund for up to 80 percent of each loan made by DCF through MSBDFA. This brings the total funding committed to DCF to $15 million.

The DCF provides long-term (up to ten years) financing for working capital, equipment, machinery, and business acquisition. Occasionally the DCF will provide startup financing, but generally it serves businesses that have operated longer than eighteen months. Businesses must provide detailed financial and accounting records to the DCF.

Loan amounts range from $5,000 to $750,000, with the average loan amount being $82,000. Loans are secured by collateral and a personal guarantee from the borrower. Businesses qualified to receive loans include retail, wholesale, manufacturing, and service industries. The DCF requires borrowers to contribute some equity.

The twelve-member governing board is made up of bankers and members of the minority business community. The seven-member investment committee includes the DCF president, senior level bank officials, and minority business owners.

The DCF staff collaborates with the Baltimore Council for Equal Business Opportunity, the Prince George's County Minority Business Resource Institute, the National Business League of Southern Maryland, and the Prince George's County Economic Development Commission to provide the technical assistance often needed by minority businesses.

Comments

The Development Credit Fund has loaned more than $7 million since its inception, resulting in the creation of an additional 440 jobs and the retention of another 54, along with business expansion and increased wage and tax bases. DCF has a default rate average of less than 7 percent.

DCF currently has $2.8 million outstanding in loans and projects that by the mid-1990s $4.5 to $5 million will be outstanding. DCF has approved eighty-one loans out of more than 400 requests.

Florida Black Business Investment Board, Tallahassee, Florida

Established by state legislation in 1987, the Florida Black Business Investment Board (FBBIB) was created to develop programs addressing black business development issues. The FBBIB, through several creative and traditional financing sources including a $5 million state trust incentive fund and matching funds from a multi-bank consortia, created the Black Business Investment Corporations (BBICs). The BBICs are an independent network of nonprofit, investment corporations governed by the FBBIB. Each BBIC has a minimum of four banks or bank holding company investors sponsoring its operations. The financial instutitions were authroized by their bank regulators to invest in the BBICs as community development corporations.

The primary goal of the BBICs is to foster and promote the growth of black businesses in Florida. The activities which they undertake reflect this goal. The BBICs are authorized to provide a full range of financial and technical assistance programs.

The governing board of each BBIC consists of bankers, black business owners, and public sector representatives. The seven member loan investment committee is comprised of both bankers and black business owners.

Program Activities

Initial capitalization totalling $10 million (state and local funds and matching bank contributions) enabled the BBIB to invest in or create six BBICs in Jacksonville, Orlando, Tampa, West Palm Beach, Miami, and Fort Lauderdale.

The BBICs have been able to develop a number of business assistance networks and entrepreneurial development programs, and they provide a number of financing instruments that enhance black economic development.

The BBICs are authorized to provide equity investments, loan guarantees, working and venture capital, leveraged buyout, and acquisition financing. BBICs also are implementing a Black Contractors Cooperative that will enable contractors to purchase at bulk rate discounts, provide bond funding, provide technical assistance for contractors, and match prospective contractors with state agencies and contracts. BBICs may be used to underwrite black contractors needing capital or support with bonding to perform on contracts with the Florida Department of Transportation (FDOT).

The BBICs also initiate "impact projects" designed to accomplish several goals. One of the most immediate is to revitalize a distressed area. BBICs work in partnership with professional developers to complete these projects. Additionally, impact projects provide retail space for black businesses.

The BBICs can provide an array of programs to assist black businesses. The programs include ongoing education and technical assistance — through its Entrepreneurial Institute — in identifying market opportunities and customers (bid matching), and a business incubator facility for startups and other small businesses. Investment centers are instituting pilot programs to launch the FBBIB's new Franchise Technical Assistance and Finance program. This program will provide the black franchisee with assistance in franchise acquisition including negotiation, financial and operational analysis.

Comments

BBICs are multifaceted organizations, each able to maintain a "local flavor" by establishing its own business programs for specific black communities.

The average size of a BBIC loan is under $60,000. Loan pricing and loan minimums are left to individual BBICs and done on a deal-by-deal basis. Each BBIC categorizes loans by risk. To date, the default rate is 4.8 percent on more than $5 million in loans.

Massachusetts Housing Investment Corporation, Boston, Massachusetts

The formal dialogue between Massachusetts bankers and community leaders began in early 1989, at a time when Boston lenders came under scrutiny by the media for two studies critical of mortgage lending patterns in the City of Boston. In the summer of 1989 the Massachusetts Bankers Association established the Affordable Housing Task Force composed of bank, city, state, and community representatives.

The mission of the Affordable Housing Task Force was to increase financing available from the banking industry for affordable housing development in Massachusetts. In addition, the Task Force sought new means of coordinating public and private resources for affordable housing. Two types of financing – debt and equity – emerged as primary needs. The Task Force devised a plan to address both debt and equity financing through one umbrella organization, the Massachusetts Housing Investment Corporation (MHIC).

Program Activities

Incorporated in July 1990, MHIC is a nonprofit corporation designed to facilitate and provide financing for housing affordable to low- and moderate-income (80 percent or less of median income households) in Massachusetts. To address both debt and equity issues, the corporation has two fundamental components – a multi-bank loan consortium and a low-income housing tax credit equity fund.

The loan consortium is a statewide, nonprofit corporation consisting of banks and savings institutions. The member institutions will capitalize the consortium up to $100 million in loan financing. The loan capital is used to supply developers across the state with debt financing for acquisition, rehabilitation, and new construction of affordable housing. The consortium concentrates on multi-family affordable housing developments which are under $5 million in size. Loan products available from the consortium include construction, mini-permanent, and permanent financing. By selling loans to the secondary market such as Fannie Mae, Freddie Mac, and insurance companies, the $100 million in the loan pool is continually recycled.

In addition to the loan pool, MHIC has a commitment of $100 million from financial institutions to invest directly in low-income housing developments. The Equity Fund utilizes the Tax Reform Act of 1986 which provides for tax credits to corporations which make direct investments in low-income housing developments. MHIC does not directly invest capital from the Equity Fund as it does with the loan consortia capital. Rather, MHIC staff reviews and analyzes low-income tax credit deals throughout the state. MHIC staff then presents and recommends sound tax credit deals to those member institutions who made commitments to the equity fund. At that point, the decision to invest in the particular deal is made by individual institutions. The Massachusetts Equity Fund provides a "one-stop shopping" alternative for developers seeking bank investors in their affordable housing developments.

MHIC earns income to meet operational costs from three primary sources. The loan pool generates income from application fees, loans fees, and a modest point spread on loan interest rates. MHIC also receives a portion of the interest earned on unused loan pool capital deposited in member banks and charges a fee (one-half to 1 percent of the total investment) for analyzing low-income tax credit deals in which members actually invest. In addition, the consortium will build up a loan loss reserve over time to cover any defaults.

Comments

As a cooperative effort on behalf of private financial institutions, MHIC addresses the needs of organizations with various interests and constraints. MHIC is a constant source of financing for nonprofit and for-profit developers endeavoring to increase the state's supply of affordable housing. Most importantly, MHIC acts in partnership with public finance agencies to leverage additional capital for affordable housing development.

Massachusetts Minority Enterprise Investment Corporation, Boston, Massachusetts

As a result of the credit needs forums held at the Federal Reserve in the summer of 1989, the Massachusetts Bankers Association created the Minority Economic Development Task Force to address the needs expressed by the minority business community. The mission of the Task Force was to identify alternatives and recommendations to help minority and disadvantaged businesses obtain credit.

The Task Force recognized that access to credit (debt and equity) and technical assistance were two of the most critical issues for minority and disadvantaged businesses. To broaden the market in terms of meeting these needs, the Task Force recommended the establishment of an intermediary organization, the Massachusetts Minority Enterprise Investment Corporation (MMEIC), a for-profit, multi-bank community development corporation (as authorized by the Office of the Comptroller of the Currency).

Program Activities

The MMEIC's mission is to increase access to bank financing for minority and disadvantaged firms through loans and equity investments. The organization will make loans in amounts between $2,500 and $250,000, concentrating on the lower-end of the market for small business loans. The small dollar size of the loans generally required by businesses in this market segment makes servicing these businesses difficult within the current banking industry. Additionally, MMEIC will work with and assist minority and disadvantaged businesses to identify and access technical and financial assistance programs to improve their management skills and business operations.

MMEIC will also identify and undertake special community impact projects such as small business incubators. In order to leverage its impact, the MMEIC will provide a full range of financial assistance in conjunction with other bank investors, public sector programs, and quasi-public development finance agencies.

A subsidiary SBA-licensed Minority Enterprise Small Business Investment Company (MESBIC), capitalized initially at $2 million, will be primarily responsible for making long-term equity investments. It will also provide subordinated debt financing to minority businesses, possibly in collaboration with MMEIC's financing activities. The Massachusetts Community Development Finance Corporation will be contracted with to provide the operations management of MESBIC.

A group of banks have committed to make investments totalling $10 million in MMEIC, of which $5 million will be invested directly in MESBIC. An additional $50 million in lines of credit will be made available from banks across the state.

Comments

MMEIC is the result of cooperative efforts on behalf of the public and private sectors. Although financial institutions are providing the initial loan capital to the corporation, MMEIC intends to use its funds to leverage further capital from other private and public institutions. In this way, MMEIC can spread risk and increase its impact.

Massachusetts Soft Second Program, Boston, Massachusetts

As part of its comprehensive statewide Community Investment Program, the Massachusetts Bankers Association implemented a "soft second" program that will initially provide $20 million in second loans to serve first-time home buyers. The loan program is a joint initiative among participating banks and state and city government. State and local government will provide funding for a loan loss reserve fund and provide support a portion of the interest costs for second loans. The second loan will be originated by the same bank that originates the first mortgage.

Soft second loans are second mortgages with reduced or "soft" interest rates. These rates are made available to low- and moderate-income first-time home buyers. The soft interest rates in conjunction with flexible underwriting criteria reduce monthly mortgage payments and initial closing costs.

Program Activities

The program will provide second loans of up to $25,000 to qualified home buyers. The terms of this loan will be flexible and allow the first mortgage amount to be reduced to 75 percent of the home's value. The program is available to moderate income individuals with incomes as low as $25,000 or below 80 percent of the area median.

The soft second loan program is expected to work in conjunction with a variety of other first mortgage products, including the GE mortgage program and individual bank-sponsored affordable home mortgage products.

Soft second mortgages will be used in combination with first mortgages that have low loan-to-value ratios of approximately 75 percent. The second mortgage is approximately 20 percent of the property's value, leaving the borrower with a 5 percent down payment.

In addition to requiring only a 5 percent down payment, mortgages structured in this manner will have low monthly payments for three primary reasons. First, mortgages with a 75 percent loan-to-value ratio do not require private mortgage insurance, thus reducing monthly payments. Second, payments on the second mortgage are phased in gradually after the first five years, with annual increases of approximately 3 percent to 5 percent. Finally, public and private funds will be used to subsidize the second mortgage loan's interest rate, typically 1 percent to 2 percent below market rates.

By underwriting mortgages structured in this way, lenders can calculate debt-to-income ratios based on the monthly mortgage payments for the first five years of the loan. Since these payments are lower than future payments, low- and moderate-income people need less income to qualify for a loan. This, combined with lower monthly payments, makes home ownership easier and more affordable.

THE COMMUNITY REINVESTMENT ACT

Comments

The Massachusetts Soft Second Program will bring home ownership to numerous low- and moderate-income families. By decreasing down payment costs, closing costs, and monthly mortgage payments, many more families will be able to achieve home ownership with the assistance of both public and private resources.

Michigan Strategic Fund, Business and Industrial Development Corporations

The Michigan Strategic Fund (MSF) was established in 1985 to increase capital for business financing. A number of its programs are directly targeted toward small and minority-owned businesses. Before instituting its programs, the MSF determined two important financing gaps that needed to be filled: moderate risk capital for companies and seed capital for entrepreneurs. The Capital Access Program and the Minority Business and Industrial Development Corporations (BIDCO) are vehicles developed to fill the moderate risk capital gap and encourage lending to companies that may not qualify for conventional bank lending. The Seed Capital Program provides financing for businesses prior to the need for technical assistance.

Program Activities

The Capital Access Program encourages banks to make business loans that do not qualify as conventional loans. Borrowers receive loans from banks who in turn receive guarantees from the program in case of default. Under the Program, the participating bank decides what loans will be made and what the terms and conditions will be. The cost of providing the guarantee is paid by the bank (25 percent), the borrower (25 percent) and the fund (50 percent). In its three year history, the program has made 225 loans, ranging from $3,000 to $800,000 with 80 percent of the loans averaging $65,000.

Licensed by the state, the Minority BIDCO Investment Program provides financial and management assistance to businesses. BIDCOs are private financial institutions capitalized by equity investments, borrowed money, and matching state funds. BIDCOs can provide flexible financing including unsecured or subordinated loans. Similar to the Capital Access Program, BIDCOs can address the moderate risk needs of many small, minority-owned businesses. Currently, the MSF has established six BIDCOs throughout Michigan.

Comments

The leveraging of BIDCO funds is one of the attractive features for participating banks. The state is capable of leveraging up to $2 million per BIDCO. BIDCOs subordinate investments to private lenders and include equity kickers. The expected return on equity investments is designed to compensate the BIDCOs for the risk taken on businesses.

BIDCOs are eligible to become approved lenders under the SBA's 7(a) loan guarantee program, which enables them to expand their source of funds for lending.

Private Programs

The product of private sector funding, private investment programs are designed to fill a niche not served by conventional banking sources. The programs provide funds for areas traditional lenders may overlook. A growing number of banks have committed to community development lending units or corporations. These programs have underwriting criteria more flexible than traditional criteria. The private sector uses various vehicles — including bank community development corporations, bank lending units, and loan consortia — to implement their lending programs.

This section looks at three private investment programs: American Security Bank, First National Bank of Chicago, and the Savings Association Mortgage Corporation.

American Security Bank, Washington, D.C.

American Security Bank created its Community Development Group in 1986. The Community Development Group operates out of the Real estate Division and was established to provide loans to projects in District of Columbia neighborhoods. Unlike some other banks, American Security did not take this action in response to a CRA challenge. Instead, top bank executives made community development lending a priority for the bank. The group expects projects to be both beneficial to the community as well as economically feasible. The purpose of the Community Development Lending Unit is to lend in areas that had "been redlined and suffered from a lack of any substantial private investment for several years."

Program Activities

In establishing its loan products, the lending group considered both the needs of the targeted areas and the types of developments they intended to finance. The products offered include lines of credit, letters of credit, acquisition loans, pre-development loans, mini-permanent loans, and permanent loans. Mini-permanent loans have terms of three to five years and are used to allow developers time to stabilize a project's cash flow.

Generally the group uses standard underwriting criteria when making loans. Its primary concern is to assess factors that affect cash flow and collateral. In light of this, the group calculates the debt service coverage ratio only for the bank's debt; accepts reserves or guarantees as debt service coverage when cash flow is minimal; and views other finance sources as project equity. In cases of little credit history or minimal financial statements borrowers must demonstrate technical capacity to conduct development.

Because of the group's willingness to finance non-traditional projects, the group works with various types of organizations. It has close ties to local government agencies, especially those with subordinate loan or rental subsidy programs. The group also frequently works with major real estate developers who have the capacity to complete larger projects. The group also establishes and maintains relationships with several minority developers and small business owners as well as with a few nonprofit organizations. And it works closely with investors in the secondary mortgage market. The group brings investors to projects in its early stages in order for the investor to understand how the project is financed and consider purchasing the long-term mortgage.

Comments

By late 1987, after only one-and-a-half years in business, American Security executives and the group's staff were pleased with the program's efforts and believed it has been good business for the bank. In that time the group made more than $100 million in loan commitments. More important, these loans were located exclusively in the District's inner-city communities. By the end of 1988 the group had made almost $200 million in loans. The group's staff also grew to nine members, six of them loan officers. Its portfolio reflects the types of development the group originally intended to undertake. Housing project developments compose 60 percent of the group's loan portfolio, while retail, commercial, and mixed-use projects make up 35 percent of the portfolio. Other activities, such as lines of credit, account for the portfolio's remaining 5 percent.

First National Bank Chicago — Chicago, Illinois

The First National Bank of Chicago established a Neighborhood Banking Division within the bank and charged it with implementing its new Neighborhood Lending Program. The Neighborhood Lending Program came about through a lending agreement with the Chicago Reinvestment Alliance, a coalition of more than thirty community-based organizations specializing in legislative lobbying, community organizing, and neighborhood development. The program was formed to address the housing and business development needs of Chicago's low- and moderate-income neighborhoods.

First National of Chicago agreed to lend $100 million through the Neighborhood Lending Program. Additionally, First Chicago Corporation, the bank holding company for First National of Chicago, and its foundation agreed to give $400,000 in grants to community groups, neighborhood-based groups, nonprofit borrowers, and technical assistance groups. It also agreed to purchase $20 million in Small Business Administration guaranteed loans from other lenders in order to free capital for further local reinvestment. The $100 million in loan money was divided into $15 million in single-family loans; $60 million in multi-family loans; $20 million in commercial and industrial loans; $5 million in mixed-use loans.

A review board was established to monitor the program and resolve continuing issues. Board responsibilities include ensuring loans that qualify as part of the $100 million loan program, that projects do not cause displacement, and that housing remains affordable according to low- and moderate-income residents. The ten-member board is composed of five representatives chosen by the Alliance and five by the bank.

Community groups are incorporated into the program by acting as members of the board, assisting in packaging loan requests, and endorsing borrowers, who must receive endorsement from at least one community group. It should be noted the bank has final authority over whether or not the loan is made. This ensures that loans meet the bank's, as well as the Alliance's, objectives for community reinvestment.

Program Activities

The purpose of the Neighborhood Lending Program is to invest the $100 million loan pool in Chicago's low- and moderate-income neighborhoods. In order to be eligible an area must have an income equal to or less than 80 percent of Chicago's median income. Loan money is designated for small business, commercial and industrial, and single and multi-family housing (both housing construction and rehabilitation). Loans are both long-term (twenty years for commercial loans and thirty years for residential loans), as well as short-term (one-year construction loans that may roll into long-term permanent loans). First National keeps its loans from this program in its portfolio. That is, it does not sell these loans to the secondary market. Community groups made this stipulation in the original lending agreement. First National finances multi-family projects for properties generally with six to eighteen units. These loans usually range from $100,000 to $600,000, although it provides loans of $1 million for larger properties.

In some cases, the income of a property supports more debt than appraisal values indicate, thanks to under-appraising — appraising property below its actual value based on perceptions of low property values for the area — in certain neighborhoods. Rehabilitation loans for these projects must be no greater than 80 percent of the post-rehabilitation property value. First National's program also works closely with other agencies to finance projects. Funds from city, state, and federal programs are used in coordination with First National's loans to finance projects that might not otherwise be feasible.

Comments

In April 1989 the Neighborhood Lending Program marked the end of its fifth year in operation. The program had only completed a little more than $75 million in lending in that time, because of the low volume of business in the program's first years. In its fourth year, the lending unit more than doubled the amount of loans it had made in the previous three years. In April 1989, First National bank announced another five-year commitment for $150 million, including $25 million from its previous commitment.

Within First National Bank, the Neighborhood Lending Unit is viewed as one of the best profit centers. In terms of default rate, the unit had one foreclosure in more than 250 loans. The lending unit is also willing to undertake complex deals. It frequently makes loans that involve community groups as well as government agencies and their resources. Although these deals are more time consuming, bank officials realize these projects would not get financed without the supplemental resources of government programs.

Savings Association Mortgage Company, California

Since 1971, the Savings Associations Mortgage Company has pooled loan capital from savings and loan institutions in California to provide financing for the development of affordable housing. Loan consortia are independent, nonprofit corporations created by their member financial institutions. Member institutions capitalize the consortium with financing specifically designated for acquisition, construction, rehabilitation, and mortgage lending for housing affordable to low- and moderate-income people. The consortium originates loans which members participate in on a pro rata basis. The consortium generates income from application fees, loan fees, and loan servicing.

Members provide loan capital to SAMCO which lends to nonprofit and profit developers of affordable housing. Once SAMCO has a qualified loan applicant, it presents the loan to members who select the loans in which they want to participate. SAMCO primarily provides permanent, ten-year adjustable rate mortgage loans for multi-family projects, cooperatives, single-room occupancy projects, homeless shelters, group homes, and reverse equity mortgages. SAMCO underwrites loans with a 75 percent loan-to-value ratio and no standard debt-service coverage ratio. In addition, SAMCO charges a $500 application fee, a 1 percent loan fee, and a 1 percent commitment fee. In its twenty year history, SAMCO has financed $275 million in affordable housing loans and incurred a 0 percent default after 1980 and a 2 percent default rate before 1980. In total, SAMCO has financed approximately 8,000 units of affordable housing.

Comments

The new bank regulatory environment is in part responsible for the recently interest in loan consortia. Federal regulators have put increased emphasis on the Community Reinvestment Act and how well financial institutions meet CRA requirements. Loan consortia provide a means for financial institutions of all sizes to meet CRA obligations. Loan consortia also enable financial institutions to participate in loans while reducing their risk of default and without increasing their administrative costs. Since most institutions do not have professional staffs skilled in this type of lending, loan consortia save tremendous amounts of financial and professional resources.

Intermediary Programs

Intermediary Programs are not initiated by the public sector nor by financial institutions. They are the work of intermediaries — private corporations whose mission it is to work with public and private institutions to promote housing and economic development. Intermediary organizations provide loans, grants, and technical assistance to community-based organizations involved in community economic development. In addition, intermediary organizations work closely with the public sector to leverage further capital for revitalization. This section, describes three such programs: the Enterprise Foundation, the Local Initiatives Support Corporation, and the Neighborhood Reinvestment Corporation.

The Enterprise Foundation, Columbia, Maryland

The Enterprise Foundation, founded in 1981, provides grants, loans, and technical assistance to community-based development organizations. The organizations it assists help low-income people find affordable housing and use the housing process as a tool to bring job training, skills workshops, and other services to low-income people.

Program Activities

The Enterprise Foundation's subsidiaries provide support and assistance for community groups across the country to create public/private partnerships for community revitalization, assist in securing project financing, and work with community groups as co-developer in low-income housing. The Foundation also helps community groups find cost-efficient ways to produce housing, revitalize neighborhoods, support grass roots organizations and promote self-help initiatives.

One subsidiary, the Enterprise Development Company, is a for-profit real estate development corporation. Profits from the Development Company help to offset the costs of other Foundation projects.

The Enterprise Social Investment Corporation (ESIC), another subsidiary, is a for-profit corporation that structures financing for low-income housing below market rates. ESIC coordinates difficult syndications for nonprofit groups and attracts equity investors to projects in need of additional funds. ESIC uses assets to develop partnerships for low-income housing. Nonprofit community-based developers secure financing from public and private sector and then develop the projects using for-profit contractors. ESIC then works with corporate investors who provide equity for the projects for a fixed stream of tax credits.

Enterprise Jobs and its local network offices provide services to assist individuals with job attainment and retention. Programs offered address problems of illiteracy, displaced workers, and at-risk youth and families.

In conjunction with the Dallas-based Center for Housing Resources (CHR), Enterprise formed the Dallas Housing Partnership (DHP). DHP is a coalition of banks, corporations, the City of Dallas, neighborhood-based housing developers, CHR and Enterprise. Since 1988, the Partnership has leveraged almost three dollars for every dollar it has committed to the production of low-income housing. DHP matches private financing with public loans provided by the Dallas Housing Fund. Fannie Mae provides a loan purchase program for all DHP conventional loans. Kraft, Inc. financed a revolving loan pool for use as working capital for acquisition, predevelopment and construction costs. A total of $4 million has been targeted for the construction of 424 new homes.

Enterprise staffs the Enterprise Jobs of Washington program in Washington, D.C. The program is funded by the Job Training Partnership Act (JTPA) and holds a contract for Tryout Youth Employment by the Washington, D.C. Private Industry Council. The program is a public-private venture aimed at training and employing inner-city youth. The program pays employers the full salary of program participants for the training period. If the employer is satisfied with the performance of the trainee, then the employer is expected to hire the trainee without further subsidy. Enterprise Jobs of Washington also offers a Pre-Employment Training Program to help job seekers with resume preparation, interview tips, and goal setting.

Comments

Enterprise Foundation believes better housing alone cannot break the cycle of poverty. With this realization, the Enterprise Foundation expanded its role and created Enterprise Jobs. Since its inception in 1984, over 12,700 unemployed individuals have been placed in jobs through the Enterprise Job Foundation Network.

The Enterprise loan fund has raised over $6 million at 3 percent. The foundation, with the nonprofit housing groups in the Enterprise network, have secured financing for more than 8,000 new or rehabilitated dwellings.

Local Initiatives Support Corporation, New York, New York

Local Initiatives Support Corporation (LISC) was founded in 1980 to help form productive alliances between community organizations and private sector organizations. LISC provides financial and technical assistance to community development corporations (CDCs) working to revitalize neighborhoods.

LISC, the largest private, nonprofit community development intermediary, operates in twenty-two cities across the country. Each location has its own LISC staff and a Local Advisory Committee, which recommends projects for funding consideration by the national LISC Board of Directors. If approved, national LISC will match funds raised by the Local Advisory Committee.

Program Activities

LISC provides technical assistance and financing for economic development, affordable housing, and other projects aimed at community revitalization. Financing is available through grants, loans, recoverable grants, and various forms of credit enhancement. LISC mobilizes funds at the national level from foundations, corporations, and financial institutions and distributes them to local LISCs. As of 1990, LISC aggregate funds total $100 million. Each local office also has fund accounts financed by local fund-raising efforts. LISC helps CDCs build working partnerships for neighborhood development.

LISC operates two subsidiaries: the National Equity Fund (NEF) and Local Initiatives Managed Assets Corporation (LIMAC). Both of these ventures expand the pool of capital available for community revitalization. NEF has successfully used low income housing tax credits to bring private companies into the community development arena. In 1989, NEF raised $77 million; since 1987, it has raised a total of $142 million. LIMAC offers secondary market financing for community development loans. LIMAC began with an initial investment of $9 million to purchase loans from LISC. Presently, LIMAC is expanding its portfolio to include bank and other intermediary originated loans. In Boston, LISC loaned $250,000 to the CDC of Boston to rehabilitate the former Baltimore Brush Company site, the last remaining undeveloped parcel in Roxbury's Crosstown Industrial Park. The main tenant is the Boston University Medical School. The CDC of Boston has its offices in the building and the balance of the space is rented to minority-owned small businesses.

In Houston, LISC is using $115,000 in grant and loan funds in combination with city funds and private resources to rehabilitate a 23-unit apartment building and convert it into ownership opportunities for existing tenants. LISC, in partnership with the city, has also provided a $150,000 loan to capitalize

Houston Neighborhood Housing Services' First Time Homebuyer Program.

In Hartford, LISC's $50,000 in revolving seed capital enabled El Hogar del Futuro, a CDC, to leverage $870,000 in low- and no-cost financing, two-thirds of which came from Connecticut's Urban Homesteading Program. Each home buyer in the six-unit "sweat equity" cooperative devoted 250 to 300 hours to the basic construction of the buildings.

In Pittsburgh, a former hotel was converted into commercial space containing 3,200 square feet of retail space and three floors of office space. The CDC, East Liberty Development, Inc., rehabilitated the building in partnership with a private developer at a total cost of $1 million. LISC provided the initial guarantee commitment of $100,000 used to raise public dollars. LISC helped secure an equity syndicator for the project and converted its own commitment to a $250,000 loan when the initial financing plan proved unfeasible.

Comments

LISC has used its funds to leverage more than $1 billion of direct investment in more than 525 CDCs and countless public-private partnerships among local businesses, governments, foundations, financial institutions, and community-based organizations. LISC has also succeeded in creating new funding sources for many community development organizations such as program-related investments (PRI).

The Neighborhood Reinvestment Corporation, Commercial and Economic Development, Washington, D.C.

Neighborhood Reinvestment's Department of Commercial and Economic Revitalization helps NeighborWorks organizations develop and implement strategies to increase employment and entrepreneurship opportunities for residents, enhance small business development, revitalize distressed commercial areas, and develop commercial facilities. The Neighborhood Reinvestment Corporation's initiatives also focus heavily on providing assistance to the Neighborhood Housing Service (NHS). NHSA is an intermediary that provides a secondary market for NHS loans. NHS and other local partnership organizations make up the NeighborWorks Network.

Three major components are part of the Commercial and Economic Development program. The components, the Commercial Loan Program, the Neighborhood Enterprise Center Program, and the Commercial District Revitalization are designed to address the specific revitalization needs of each neighborhood.

Program Activities

The Anchorage NHS, Inc. has helped facilitate the redevelopment of a deteriorated commercial corridor through its commercial loan program and a long-term development plan. The development strategy, implemented in 1985, includes business development programs, marketing campaigns, and a gap financing program. Since its inception, reinvestment totalling almost $60 million has been secured and more than fifteen buildings have been renovated, one new building constructed, sixteen new businesses attracted, and eight existing businesses expanded.

The NHS of Kenosha, Inc., in Kenosha, Wisconsin, is in the process of revitalizing a commercial district experiencing disinvestment and decline. The area is perceived as a high crime district with poor access and a lack of variety and physical appeal. A market study of the area helped the NHS of Kenosha to identify business development opportunities, plan physical improvements, and develop merchandising and marketing strategies. The area was established as a Business Improvement District (BID). Staffing for the management of the commercial district, leasing and business recruitment, and promotion is supported by the revenue generated by the BID.

The NHS of Kenosha developed a commercial loan program with two local financial institutions. The revolving loan fund provides tandem loans at below market rates for physical renovations or business expansions. Since the program started, a block containing ten commercial units has been renovated and two businesses expanded.

The Neighborhood Enterprise Center Program (NEC) is a pilot program designed to facilitate economic empowerment within disadvantaged communities, particularly among minorities and women. The program focuses on micro-enterprises and offers participants a support network, peer group lending system, training, and other programs designed to meet the needs of each particular area.

Each NEC includes a local financial institution partner that provides capital for the NEC loan program at below-market interest rates. Credit enhancement is provided in the form of a partial guarantee fund. The NEC makes loans of $10,000 or less to micro-enterprises.

In Pasadena, California, the Neighborhood Enterprise Center is targeted to minority whose child care responsibilities keep them from conventional employment.

Commercial District Revitalization often includes a commercial loan program as part of the strategy. The strategy is tailored to the specific needs of the local community, but involves these elements business development, commercial property rehabilitation and development, commercial district management, public improvements, and marketing and promotion strategies.

Comments

Commercial and economic development programs have been initiated in more than thirty NeighborWorks neighborhoods, resulting in more than $90 million of reinvestment. To date, more than 300 businesses have been expanded, more than 400 commercial buildings have been rehabilitated, and considerably more than 1,000 jobs have been created or retained.

The Community Reinvestment Act

SEC.801. This title may be cited as the "Community Reinvestment Act of 1977."

SEC.802(a) The Congress finds that —

> (1) regulated financial institutions are required by law to demonstrate that their deposit facilities serve the convenience and needs of the communities in which they are chartered to do business;

> (2) the convenience and needs of communities include the need for credit services; and

> (3) regulated financial institutions have continuing and affirmative obligation to help meet the credit needs of the local communities in which they are chartered.

> > (b) It is the purpose of this title to require each appropriate Federal financial supervisory agency to use its authority when examining financial institutions, to encourage such institutions to help meet the credit needs of the local communities in which they are chartered consistent with the safe and sound operation of such institutions.

SEC.803. For the purpose of this title —

> (1) the term "appropriate Federal financial supervisory agency" means —

> > (A) the Comptroller of the Currency which respect to national banks;

> > (B) the Board of Governors of the Federal Reserve System with respect to State chartered banks which are members of the Federal Reserve System and bank holding companies;

(C) the Federal Deposit Insurance Corporation with respect to state chartered banks and savings banks which are not members of the Federal Reserve System and which are insured by the Corporation; and

(D) the Federal Home Loan Bank Board with respect to institutions the deposits of which are insured by the Federal Savings and Loan Insurance Corporation and to savings and loan holding companies.

(2) the term "regulated financial institution" means an insured bank as defined in Section 3 of Federal Deposit Insurance Act or an insured institution as defined in Section 401 of the National Housing Act; and

(3) the term "application for a deposit facility" means an application to the appropriate Federal financial supervisory agency otherwise required under Federal law or regulations thereunder for:

(A) a charter for a national bank of Federal savings and loan association;

(B) deposit insurance in connection with a newly chartered State bank, savings bank, saving and loan association or similar institutions;

(C) the establishment of a domestic branch or other facility with the ability to accept deposits of a regulated financial institutions;

(D) the relocation of the home office or a branch office of a regulated financial institutions;

(E) the merger or consolidation with, or the acquisition of the assets, or the assumption of the liabilities of a regulated financial institution requiring approval under Section 18(C) of the Federal Deposit Insurance Act or under regulations issued under the authority of title IV of the National Housing Act; or

(F) the acquisition of shares in, or the assets of, a regulated financial institutions requiring approval under section 3 of the Bank Holding Company Act of 1956 or Section 408(e) of the National Housing Act.

SEC.804. In connection with its examination of a financial institutions, the appropriate Federal financial supervisory agency shall:

(1) assess the institution's record of meeting the credit needs of the entire community, including low and moderate income neighborhoods, consistent with the safe and sound operation of such institutions; and

(2) take such record into account in its evaluation of an application for a deposit facility by such institutions.

SEC.805. Each appropriate Federal financial supervisory agency shall include in its annual report to the Congress a section outlining the actions it has taken to carry out its responsibilities under this title.

SEC.806. Regulations to carry out the purposes of this title shall be published by each appropriate Federal financial supervisory agency, and shall take effect no later than 390 days after the date of enactment of this title.

Joint Statement of the Federal Financial Supervisory Agencies Regarding the Community Reinvestment Act (Selected Sections)

Federal Reserve Board
Comptroller of the Currency
Federal Home Loan Bank Board
Federal Deposit Insurance Corporation

INTRODUCTION

In light of the significant developments that have occurred in the financial institutions industry since enactment of the Community Reinvestment Act of 1977 (CRA), the Board of Governors of the Federal Reserve System, the Federal Deposit Insurance Corporation, the Office of the Comptroller of the Currency, and the Federal Home Loan Bank Board ("the Agencies") have revised the 1980 Community Reinvestment Act Information Statement. The revisions in this Joint Statement are intended to take advantage of the experience the Agencies, financial institutions, and community members have gained over the years in developing approaches to ensure that the requirements and purposes of the CRA are met. This revised Statement provides guidance regarding the types of policies and procedures that the Agencies believe financial institutions should have in place in order to fulfill their responsibilities under the CRA on an ongoing basis and the procedures the Agencies will use during the application process to review an institution's CRA compliance and performance.

Under the CRA, the Agencies are required, when considering certain applications involving a federally insured financial institution ("financial institution"), to take into account the institution's record of helping to meet the credit needs of its entire community, including low- and moderate-income neighborhoods.

Given this responsibility, the Agencies want to assure that potential applicants, and those who may wish to comment on an applicant's CRA record, know what is expected of a financial institution under the CRA and of participants during the application process.

The Agencies believe the clarification provided in this Statement will help applicants and others who wish to comment on applications to provide promptly the information necessary to permit the Agencies to address CRA issues in a timely fashion in accordance with the schedules required under relevant federal statutes and regulations. The Agencies wish to emphasize their belief that the goals of the CRA are best accomplished when financial institutions make meeting their responsibilities under the statute a part of their routine management and operational structure. Thus, the Agencies expect applicants to have addressed their responsibilities under the CRA well before they submit an application.

BACKGROUND

The CRA was enacted in 1977 against a backdrop of concern over unfair treatment of prospective borrowers by financial institutions and over unwarranted geographic differences in their lending patterns. In the CRA, Congress reaffirmed that every financial institution has a continuing and affirmative obligation consistent with its safe and sound operation to help meet the credit needs of its entire community, including low- and moderate-income neighborhoods. The CRA states that its purpose is to require each federal financial supervisory agency to use its authority when conduction examinations to encourage the financial institutions it supervises to help meet those needs. To this end, the Community Reinvestment Act provides:

In connection with its examination of a financial institution, the appropriate... agency shall

(1) assess the institution's record of meeting the credit needs of its entire community, including low- and moderate-income neighborhoods, consistent with the safe and sound operation of [the] institution; and

(2) take such record into account in its evaluation of an application ... by such an institution. 12 U.S.C. §2903.

Simply stated, the CRA and the implementing regulations place upon all financial institutions, whether wholesale or retail, urban or rural, an affirmative responsibility to treat the credit needs of low- and moderate-income members of their communities as they would any other market for services that the institution has decided to serve. As with any other targeted market, financial institutions are expected to ascertain credit needs and demonstrate their response to those needs.

The Agencies believe that the CRA intends financial institutions to help meet the credit needs of their communities in a positive, ongoing way that recognizes the institution's assessment of its relevant market and is consistent with the safe and sound operation of the institution. This responsibility under the CRA may be met in a variety of ways, including lending for business, agriculture, education, consumer, home purchase, and home improvement purposes, and to finance state and local governments. The CRA was not intended to limit an institution's discretion to develop the types of products and services that it believes are best suited to its expertise and business objectives and to the needs of its particular community, as long as the institution's program is consistent with the objectives of the CRA. Nor is it the purpose of this Statement to establish specific lending requirements or programs for financial institutions subject to the CRA.

This Statement provides guidance, in part, by describing the types of activities that Agencies have found to fulfill a financial institution's responsibilities under CRA. Because the needs of communities vary, the Agencies recognize that the examples outlined in this Statement will not be appropriate for every institution or for every community.

GUIDELINES FOR DEVELOPING AN EFFECTIVE CRA PROCESS

Because the credit needs of individual communities differ, the Agencies will consider the process by which a financial institution defines the community it serves, determines its credit needs, including its low- and moderate-income areas, and takes steps to help meet those needs through appropriate and prudent lending. The Agencies believe the appropriate consideration should be given to an institution that makes ongoing efforts to ascertain the needs of its entire community, develops products and services that are responsive to those needs, and markets those products and services throughout the community. An active program of management involvement, policy oversight, and regular review is most likely to assure that the products and services the institution chooses to offer will meet community credit needs, be adjusted when those needs change, and be available to all segments of the community.

The experience of the Agencies indicates that an effective CRA process must include methods to ascertain community needs on an ongoing basis through outreach efforts to local governments, businesses, and community members and organizations. This ascertainment effort should include a system that both facilitates dialogue with these individuals and groups and enables them to communicate their concerns to an officer of the financial institution with CRA responsibilities. To be effective, the process must include methods to incorporate findings regarding community credit needs into the development of products and services that the institutions decides to offer to help meet these needs.

The CRA plan should include marketing and advertising programs for lending products and services that are responsive to the needs of the community and that will inform and stimulate awareness of those products and services throughout the community, including low- and moderate-income areas. The plan should also include periodic analysis of the disposition of loan applications to ensure that potential borrowers are treated in a fair and nondiscriminatory manner.

The duty to coordinate and monitor the CRA process should be assigned to a senior officer or a committee charged with the responsibility to report periodically to the board of directors about the institution's CRA efforts, performance and areas for improvement, where appropriate. An employee training program should be established. This program should contain information about those policies of the institution designed to help meet community credit needs, including the needs of low- and moderate-income areas and small businesses. Procedures should be implemented to assure that files are maintained, as required by agency regulations, for purposes of receiving public comments and for reviewing and responding to these comments.

Regardless of how an institution organizes itself to implement such a plan, seeing that the institution has taken the steps necessary to help meet its community's credit needs is the responsibility of the entire organization, beginning with its board of directors and continuing through its line management.

Once a financial institution has established an effective CRA process, it must assure that its CRA statement accurately reflects that types of lending and other services that it will offer to the community. This statement must be reviewed at least annually to ensure its accuracy. The services that the institution chooses to offer should be clearly articulated, reasonably related to community credit needs, and distributed in a fair and nondiscriminatory manner in keeping with an institution's general approach to its business. A financial institution need not offer every financial service in order to meet its CRA responsibilities; however, the Agencies expect that institutions will offer the types of credit listed in their CRA statement throughout their delineated communities.

SPECIFIC ELEMENTS OF AN EFFECTIVE CRA PROCESS

Within the general framework discussed above, institutions have substantial leeway in developing specific policies and programs to meet their CRA responsibilities. The actual steps taken by an institution will of necessity depend upon a number of factors, including the size of the institution, its business strategy and objectives, and the size, nature and needs of the community involved. For example, the specific steps taken by a small rural institution to meet its CRA responsibilities may be quite different from those required of a major metropolitan institution.

Based upon the experience of the Agencies, institutions with the most effective programs for meeting their CRA responsibilities and for assuring that their services reach low- and moderate-income segments of the community will have taken many of the following steps:

- implemented policies, including the use of more flexible lending criteria, consistent with safe and sound practices, to provide the types of loans and services described in the institution's CRA statement on a more widespread basis;

- increased efforts to make loans to help meet identified credit needs within the community, such as those for home mortgages, home improvement and small business. This may include participation in various government-insured lending programs, such as FHA-insured or VA-guaranteed mortgage loans and SBA loans, and participation in other types of lending programs such as high-loan-to-value-ration conventional mortgage loans with private mortgage insurance;

- implemented and advertised the availability of services of benefit to low- and moderate-income persons, such as cashing government checks or offering low-cost checking accounts;

- created and implemented advertising and marketing efforts through, for example, newspapers, radio, television and brochures designed to inform low- and moderate-income groups (in languages other than English, where appropriate) of available loan and deposit services;

- expanded officer call programs to include targeted groups, such as small business owners and real estate agency in low- and moderate-income neighborhoods, in order to inform them of available credit services;

- established a process involving all levels of management in efforts to contact governmental leaders, economic development practitioners, businesses and business associations, and community organizations to discuss the financial services that are needed by the community;

■ developed systems to provide assistance to customers or potential customers regarding federal, state or local assistance programs to small businesses, or for housing or other similar community needs;

■ adopted a written corporate policy concerning branch closings which contains provisions for appropriate notice, analysis of the impact of the closing on the local community, and efforts that may be made to minimize any adverse effects;

■ participated in or provided assistance to community development programs or projects, such as Neighborhood Housing Services programs, small business programs encouraged by the Small Business Administration or Economic Development Administration, or Community Development Block Grant programs;

■ established a community development corporation;

■ funded a small business investment corporation or created a minority small business investment corporation;

■ made lines of credit and other financing available, within prudent lending principles, to non-profit developers of low-income housing and small business developments, for low-income multi-family rehabilitation and new construction projects, and/or provided a secondary market for non-profit developer paper;

■ underwritten or invested in state municipal bonds; or

■ in the case of members of the Federal Home Loan Bank System, participated actively in the FHLBB Community Investment Fund program.

Finally, to enhance CRA performance, some financial institutions have chosen to establish special or pilot lending programs earmarked for low- and moderate-income neighborhoods, consistent with safe and sound lending practices. While the Agencies support such activity, the scope of any such program is properly addressed by the financial institution itself, taking into account its own expertise and financial capabilities. This is particularly true of any targeted goals established for such a program, which may represent a statement of the financial institution's expectations of services to be provided based upon actual loan demand, market conditions, and other similar factors. The Agencies will continue to consider favorably financial-institution leadership in concerted efforts to improve low- and moderate-income areas in the community and participation by financial institutions in public and private partnerships to promote economic and community development efforts.

The examples described above illustrate specific steps that have been taken, in particular by larger financial organizations operating in urban communities, to help meet the credit needs of all segments of those communities. Smaller financial organizations operating in primary rural communities may nonetheless find some of these examples helpful in designing CRA policies that would meet the needs of their communities.

EXPANDED CRA STATEMENT

Financial institutions are currently required by agency regulations to prepare a CRA statement describing the community served by the institution and listing the types of credit offered by the institution to the community and encouraged to describe their CRA efforts in this statement. This statement must be reviewed by the board of directors of the institution at lease on an annual basis. As noted above, an effective CRA process should also include management review and oversight of the institution's policies and performance on a regular basis.

The Agencies believe that it would be especially useful for a financial institution, in connection with the preparation and periodic review of its CRA statement, to expand the CRA statement to include a description of the institution's CRA performance. The CRA regulations of the Agencies currently encourage financial institutions to incorporate this type of description in their CRA statements. This description includes the institution's efforts to ascertain the credit needs of its community and to communicate with members of the community regarding those needs, and the steps taken by the institution, including through special credit-related programs, to help meet the community's credit needs. The CRA statement also provides a readily available vehicle for financial institutions to describe the marketing and advertising programs used by the institution to inform the community of the institution's services, and any other steps, such as those outlines in this Statement, that have been taken by the institution to implement its CRA policies. The institution may also find it useful to include a summary of the results of its internal CRA review and a summary of the documentation collected by the institution regarding its CRA performance.

An expanded CRA statement along the lines suggested in existing agency regulations can be a particularly effective part of the institution's outreach efforts to the community. This type of statement would also focus, on an ongoing basis, the attention of both the institution's management and the public on the financial institution's efforts to meet its responsibilities under the CRA and on any areas identified by the institution for improvement.

The Agencies also believe that an expanded CRA statement would present a suitable framework outside the applications process for public comment regarding an institution's CRA record. Under existing rules, public comments received by an institution regarding its CRA performance must be maintained in a public comment file with the institution's CRA statement. These public comments provide the institution with an opportunity to identify areas of public concern regarding its CRA performance and to consider any steps that the institution may find appropriate to address these concerns. The Agencies may then review these comments and the steps taken by the institution to address the comments during the CRA examination of the institution rather than through the application process.

The Agencies strongly encourage financial institutions to expand their CRA statement to include a description of the institution's CRA performance in connection with the institution's review of its CRA record. The Federal Reserve Board and the FHLBB also strongly encourage holding companies, as part of the system-wide review and oversight by the holding company of the CRA performance of its subsidiary financial institutions, to ensure tat their CRA statements are expanded in this way. The Agencies recognize that the CRA statement would vary in complexity and scope depending on the size, resources, and location of the institution.

COMMUNICATION IN ADVANCE OF THE APPLICATION PROCESS

Just as financial institutions are expected to communicate with their local communities on an ongoing basis regarding credit needs, community organizations and other members of the public are strongly encouraged to bring comments regarding an institution's CRA performance to the attention of the institution and the appropriate supervisory agency at the earliest possible time. Interested persons are encouraged not to wait to present their comments through a protest to an application.

Prompt submission of comments regarding an institution's CRA record provides the institution and examiners with a timely opportunity to evaluate the matter and permits the institution to correct any deficiencies -an opportunity that may not be as effectively utilized under the time constraints of the application process. The CRA regulations of the Agencies establish a comment procedure at the financial institution for this purpose, and the Agencies strongly encourage use of this process. The Agencies expect that financial institutions will investigate promptly all complaints and place a high priority on correcting any deficiencies.

The Agencies will consider any comments submitted to an institution through this comment procedure, as well as any action or response that the institution deems appropriate, in the evaluation of the institution's CRA performance. In this regard, when considering public comments received during the applications process concerning the CRA record of a particular institution, the Agencies will take into account whether the institution has provided to the public an expended CRA statement that, as discussed above, describes the efforts made by the institution to help meet the credit needs of its community. The Agencies may also consider whether the commenter has submitted comments to the institution in response to the institution's CRA statement outside of the applications process. However, comments will be carefully weighed regardless of their timing, as long as submitted within the periods specified in the rules of the appropriate reviewing Agency.

CONCLUSION

The Agencies consider it important that financial institutions act effectively to meet the requirements of the CRA in a positive and ongoing manner. The Agencies believe that this can be done in a way that will not only benefit local communities, but also will be consistent with the safe and sound operation of financial institutions. Doing so, however, requires managerial effort, oversight and review. An institution's processes for meeting the credit needs of its community must reflect an understanding of those needs and take into account changes that may occur in the community's credit needs. By applying sound management techniques to the challenges presented by the CRA, financial institutions can be agents of positive change for the cities, towns and rural areas of this country -thereby benefiting themselves as well as the communities that they serve.

William W. Wiles
March 21, 1989

Uniform Interagency Community Reinvestment Act Final Guidelines for Disclosure of Written Evaluations and Revised Assessment Rating System

April 25, 1990

The new Section 807 of the Community Reinvestment Act (CRA) requires that the appropriate Federal depository institution regulatory agency shall prepare a written evaluation of the institution's record of meeting the credit needs of its entire community, including low- and moderate-income neighborhoods. Section 807, in addition, requires that these written evaluations have a public and confidential section.

The procedures detailed below will be followed by the supervisory agencies and the financial institutions to disclose to the public an institution's CRA performance evaluation.

Disclosure by the Financial Institution

The appropriate supervisory agency will prepare an institution's CRA performance evaluation upon completion of CRA examinations commencing on and after July 1, 1990 and will transmit the evaluation to the institution at the time it send the written CRA examination report. The CRA performance evaluation will be a separate document, distinct from the examination report, thereby maintaining the confidentiality of the examination report and complying with the statutory mandates.

This approach will provide convenient access by the public to each institution's evaluation as it will:

■ Ensure public access to the evaluation in communities served by the institution.

■ Be consistent with other requirements already imposed on financial institutions by current CRA regulations (e.g., maintenance of CRA statements and public file, posting of CRA notice).

■ Facilitate comparisons by the public of the CRA statement prepared by the institution with the evaluation prepared by the supervisory agency. Indirectly, it could encourage development of well documented, expanded CRA statements by each institution, as recommended by the Statement of the Federal Financial Supervisory Agencies Regarding the Community Reinvestment Act. See 54 Fed. Reg. 13742 (April 5, 1989).

■ Help encourage greater attention by the institution's board of directors, management and employees to the institution's CRA performance in all community areas served by local depository offices.

The financial institution would be required to:

■ Make its most current CRA performance evaluation available to the public within 30 business days of its receipt;

■ At a minimum, place the evaluation in the institution's CRA public file located at the head office and a designated office in each local community;

■ Add the following language to the institution's CRA public notice that is posted in each depository facility, within 30 business days of receipt of the first evaluation:

> "You may obtain the public section of our most recent CRA Performance Evaluation, which was prepared by (name of agency), at (address of head office) [if the institution has more than one local community, each office (other than off-premises electronic deposit facilities) in that community shall also include the address of the designated office for that community.]"

■ Provide a copy of its current evaluation to the public, upon request, and will be authorized to charge a fee not to exceed the cost of reproduction and mailing (if applicable);

The format and content of the institution's evaluation, as prepared by its supervisory agency, may not be altered or abridged in any manner. The institution is encouraged to include its response to the evaluation in its CRA public comment file.

Format and Content of Required Written Evaluation

In addressing the format and content of disclosures, the agencies believe two considerations should be emphasized. First, the agencies will strive to achieve consistency in preparing the evaluations. Consistency will facilitate public understanding of evaluations and promote a common understanding of CRA. A common understanding shared by community groups, regulators, and depository institutions regarding CRA should result in reasonable expectations and constructive dialogue with respect to CRA issues.

Second, the language used in preparing the CRA evaluations should be simple and concise. Evaluations should be written in a manner understandable to the public. Acronyms, technical banking or regulatory terminology, and unexplained banking concepts should not be used.

Uniform Format

Because of the need for confidential treatment of the examination report, the CRA evaluation will be prepared as a stand-alone document, that may be extracted from the CRA examination report, eliminating information precluded by statute or deemed by the agencies to be confidential. The relevant statutory provisions read as follows:

> "(c) CONFIDENTIAL SECTION OF REPORT -
>
>> (1) Privacy of Named Individuals. The confidential section of the written evaluation shall contain all references that identify any customer of the institution, any employee or officer of the institution, or any person or organization that has provided information in confidence to a Federal or state depository institutions regulatory agency.
>>
>> (2) Topics Not Suitable for Disclosure. The confidential section shall also contain any statements obtained or made by the appropriate Federal depository institutions regulatory agency in the course of an examination which, in the judgment of the agency, are too sensitive or speculative in nature to disclose to the institution or the public.
>>
>> (3) Disclosure To Depository Institution. The confidential section may be disclosed, in whole or part, to the institution, if the appropriate Federal depository institutions regulatory agency determines that such disclosure will promote the objectives of

this Act. However, disclosure under this paragraph shall not identify a person or organization that has provided information in confidence to a Federal or State depository institutions regulatory agency."

(Sec. 1212, FIRREA, Pub. L. No. 101-73, 103 Stat. 183)

Content of Evaluation

To facilitate understanding the CRA, it is desirable to preface the evaluation with background information outlining the general purposes of the CRA and explaining the evaluation.

Evaluations will be based only on the examiners' findings from the time the examination starts until the CRA Performance Evaluation receives the final approval from the appropriate supervisory agency. The agencies will not include in the CRA Performance Evaluation an institution's verbal or written response to CRA examination findings that are received after the supervisory office has given its final approval to the examiner's Evaluation. The agencies encourage, but do not require, financial institutions to include their response to the evaluation in their CRA Public File.

Evaluation Format

To ensure maximum consistency, the agencies will use a standard format. The evaluation will consist of four distinct sections:

Section I Cover Page and General Information Page

Section II Ratings Information Identification of Ratings

Section III The Institution's Specific Rating and Narrative Discussing Performance under the Assessment Factors and Supporting Facts

Section IV Additional Information

Section I — Cover Page and General Information

The cover page will include:

1. The date of the evaluation.

2. The name and address of the institution.

3. The name and address of the supervisory agency.

4. A cautionary note stating that the CRA evaluation is not an assessment of the financial condition of the institution.

A standard "General Information" page will address the purpose of both the CRA and the public written evaluation. It will also provide a statement on the basis for the rating.

Section II — Rating Information

This page will contain the four ratings specified in section 807 of the CRA. A brief description of each rating will precede the presentation of the particular institution's rating and will provide a standard for comparison. For example, presentation of a "Needs to Improve" rating will clearly be identified as not being the worst possible rating.

Section III — Discussion of Institution's Performance

This page will contain:

- The rating for the institution resulting from the examination.

- The performance categories will be listed with the relevant assessment factors, as written in the regulation, spelled out and followed by a narrative supporting the conclusion under each factor.

Section IV. — Additional Information

This section may include any other relevant information that does not appropriately fit in other sections, such as the Metropolitan Statistical Area (MSA) in which the institution is located, the location of branches, and the location of the appropriate HMDA depository.

Federal Regulatory Agencies

Board of Governors of the Federal Reserve System
Division of Consumer and Community Affairs
20th & Constitution Avenue, NW
Washington, D.C. 20551; (202) 452-3585.

Federal Deposit Insurance Corporation
Office of Consumer Affairs
550 Seventeenth Street, NW
Washington, D.C. 20429; (202) 898-3536.

Office of Thrift Supervision
Division of Compliance Programs
1700 G Street, NW
Washington, D.C. 20552; (202) 785-5442.

Office of the Comptroller of the Currency
Compliance Management
490 L'Enfant Plaza, SW
Washington, D.C. 20219; (202) 287-4169.

CRA Rating System

The chart on the following pages presents a full listing of the performance categories and assessment factors used by the bank regulatory agencies to rate bank CRA performance. Becoming familiar with the rating system can help you work with local banks to meet your community's need for investment and credit and banking services and their need to comply with the CRA requirements.

Chart © American Bankers Association. Reprinted with permission All rights reserved.

CRA Rating System

PERFORMANCE CATEGORIES AND ASSESSMENT FACTORS	Outstanding	✔	Satisfactory	✔	Needs to Improve	✔	Substantial Noncompliance	✔
I. Ascertainment of Community Credit Needs								
(A) Activities to ascertain credit needs and efforts to communicate with the community								
■ contact with individuals and groups	Ongoing, meaningful		Regular contact		Limited contact		Few if any	
■ contact with government officials and community leaders	Ongoing		Regular contact		Limited contact		Few if any	
■ participation in public programs	Active		Some effort		Marginal effort		Nominal or none	
■ relationships with private nonprofit developers and financial intermediaries resulting in public-private partnerships	Established and productive		Regular contact		Lack of productive contact		Few if any	
■ collection and analysis of local demographic data regarding lending activities	Regularly collected and analyzed		Periodically reviewed		Occasionally considered or analyzed		Unaware or ignorant of	
■ responsiveness of board of directors and senior management in addressing community credit needs through product development and lending	Proactive attitude and highly responsive		Satisfactory		Limited		Rare or never	
■ senior management review of lending services	Systematic and regular		Informal		Infrequent		Rare or never	
■ credit products structured or varied to meet identified needs; may include government-insured and publicly sponsored programs	Well-suited products, including those that make use of government-insured or publicly sponsored programs		Reasonably suited products, including those that make use of government-insured and publicly sponsored programs		May not meet needs; insignificant participation in government-insured and publicly sponsored programs		Rare or none; nominal or no participation in government-insured and publicly sponsored programs	
■ board of directors and senior management efforts to explore and offer conventional products with special features and more flexible lending criteria within safe and sound practices	Demonstrated willingness		May explore and offer		Limited effort		Little or no effort	
(C) Board of directors participation in formulating policies and reviewing institution's CRA performance								
■ extent of participation and review	Integral part of CRA process and activities		Generally involved		Limited involvement		Rare or no involvement	

continued

CRA Rating System *(continued)*

PERFORMANCE CATEGORIES AND ASSESSMENT FACTORS	Outstanding	✔	Satisfactory	✔	Needs to Improve	✔	Substantial Noncompliance	✔
■ CRA program with goals, objectives, and methodology for self-assessment	Formal, written program		Articulated and generally understood, but possibly not explicitly reflected in formal program		Inadequate program		No program	
■ policy oversight of CRA activities	Active oversight		Oversight exercised		Some oversight		Little or no oversight	
■ review of CRA activities and performance	Regular review		Occasional review		Infrequent review		Rare or no review	
■ analysis of disposition of loan applications to check fairness and nondiscrimination compliance	Annual or more frequent analysis		At least annual analysis		Only limited analysis		Rare or no analysis	
■ activities designed to develop, improve, and enhance local community	Personally involved		Some involvement		Limited involvement		Little, if any, involvement	
■ prudent but innovative underwriting criteria to address community credit needs	Consistent support		Consideration given		May be reluctant to consider		Reluctant to consider	
■ CRA training of personnel	Active support		Adequate support		Limited support		Little, if any, support	
■ Expanded CRA Statement adoption	Yes; includes self-assessment and documentation of performance		Yes, but might not be fully descriptive of institution's performance		No		No	
■ CRA technical regulatory requirements being met	Effective efforts to ensure compliance		Generally ensures		Lax		Rarely or never	
II. Marketing and Types of Credit Extended (B) Extent of marketing and special credit-related programs								
■ marketing and advertising programs	Sound programs, approved, reviewed, and monitored by senior management and board		Adequate, but exist outside formal oversight of senior management and board		Limited oversight by senior management and board		If exist, are inadequate	
■ programs inform all segments of the community of products and services offered	Yes		Designed to inform		May require revision or expansion		No	
■ advertisements of credit services throughout the community	Designed to stimulate awareness		Ads carried in widely circulated local media		Ads designed only to promote institution's image as provider of products and services		No	

continued

CRA Rating System *(continued)*

PERFORMANCE CATEGORIES AND ASSESSMENT FACTORS	✔	Outstanding	✔	Satisfactory	✔	Needs to Improve	✔	Substantial Noncompliance	✔
■ use of special advertisement media aimed at particular segments of community		Yes		Additional targeted advertising may be needed		No		No	
■ maintenance of advertising and marketing records		Complete, readily available		Adequate		Limited		Insufficient	
■ review of advertising and marketing programs to ensure compliance with applicable laws and regulations		Routinely reviewed		Occasionally reviewed		Infrequently reviewed		Rarely or never reviewed	
■ personnel involvement to assist individuals and groups applying for credit		Routinely provide assistance		Generally provide assistance		Limited effort		Little, if any, effort	
(I) Origination or purchase of loans within community									
■ meeting identified community credit needs through origination and purchase of loans		Affirmatively addresses a substantial portion of identified needs		Addresses a significant portion of needs		Marginal		Minimal	
■ lending levels in response to community credit needs		Exceptional responsiveness to most pressing needs		General responsiveness		Marginal responsiveness		Little, if any, responsiveness	
■ number of loans within delineated community		Substantial majority		Significant volume		Significant volume may be outside delineated community		Substantial majority outside delineated community	
■ loan volume relative to institution's resources and community's needs		Exceeds expectations		Adequate		Low		Excessively low	
■ CRA Statement lists credit products available from the institution		Correctly listed		Majority correctly listed		Not accurately listed		Statement is materially inaccurate	
(J) Participation in governmentally insured, guaranteed, or subsidized loan programs									
■ approach to meeting identified community credit needs		Assumes leadership role		Generally takes some steps		Sometimes becomes involved		Rarely or never involved	
■ level of participation		Affirmatively participates		Frequently participates		Infrequently participates		Rarely or never participates	

continued

CRA Rating System (continued)

PERFORMANCE CATEGORIES AND ASSESSMENT FACTORS	✔	Outstanding	✔	Satisfactory	✔	Needs to Improve	✔	Substantial Noncompliance	✔
III. Geographic distribution and record of opening and closing offices									
(*) Reasonableness of delineated community		Meets CRA purpose and does not exclude low- and moderate-income areas		Meets CRA purpose and does not exclude low- and moderate-income areas		Delineation unreasonable and may exclude some low- and moderate-income areas; delineation guidelines need revision		Delineation unreasonable and excludes low- and moderate-income areas; delineation guidelines need substantial revision	
*not included as one of the 12 assessment factors, but considered under this category.									
(E) Geographic distribution of credit extensions, applications, and denials									
■ geographic distribution within delineated community		Documented analysis reflects reasonable penetration of all segments of community		Reasonable penetration of all segments of community		Unjustified, disproportionate pattern within delineated community compared with outside community, or regarding distribution within community		Unreasonable lending pattern inside and outside delineated community	
■ procedures formulated to identify geographic distribution		Yes		N/A		N/A		N/A	
■ geographic data documented and used by board and senior management to establish policies, products and services, and marketing plans		Yes		May be documented and used		N/A		N/A	
■ awareness of board and senior management of geographic distribution		N/A		N/A		May be unaware		Disregards	
■ review by board and senior management of lending policies and practices and effect on geographic distribution		N/A		N/A		Inadequate or no review		N/A	
■ corrective action on previously identified unreasonable lending patterns		N/A		N/A		Inadequate or no action		Limited or no action	
■ loan policies and procedures impact on local community		N/A		N/A		N/A		Contain restrictions that adversely affect loan availability	

continued

CRA Rating System *(continued)*

PERFORMANCE CATEGORIES AND ASSESSMENT FACTORS	Outstanding	Satisfactory	Needs to Improve	Substantial Noncompliance
(G) Record of opening and closing offices and providing services				
■ accessibility of offices to all segments of the community	Readily accessible	Reasonably accessible	Difficult to access	Limited access
■ accommodation through business hours and services	Tailored to convenience and needs; ongoing review	Reviewed periodically to assure accommodation	May be inconvenient and infrequently reviewed	Inconsistent and rarely if ever reviewed
■ assessment of potential adverse impact of office closings	Detailed assessment prior to closing, including consultation with community members	Adequate, including contacts with community members	Inadequate; needs revision or expansion	Rare or none
■ record of opening and closing offices as it affects local community, particularly low- and moderate-income areas	No adverse impact	Level of service available in low- and moderate-income areas not adversely affected	Adverse impact; may be unintentional	Continuing pattern of adverse impact
IV. Discrimination and Other Illegal Credit Practices **(D) Practices to discourage applications for types of credit set forth in CRA Statement**				
■ solicitation of credit applications from all segments of community	Affirmatively solicits; strong focus on low- and moderate-income areas	Generally solicits from all segments of community	Possibility of isolated, illegal discouraging or prescreening	Rarely, if ever, considers credit applications from all segments of community; volume of applications from low- or moderate-income areas low or nonexistent
■ board of directors and senior management development of policies, procedures, and training programs to prevent illegal discouragement and prescreening of applicants	Effectively assures absence of illegal discouragement or prescreening of applicants	Adequate; minor revision or expansion may be required	Inadequate; requires significant revision or expansion	Nonexistent or needs substantial revision
■ adequacy of review and reporting mechanisms to assure nondiscriminatory policies, procedures, and training programs	Regularly assessed	Periodically assessed	Improvement needed	Inadequate and requires substantial revision; or no mechanisms exist

continued

CRA Rating System (continued)

PERFORMANCE CATEGORIES AND ASSESSMENT FACTORS	Outstanding	✔	Satisfactory	✔	Needs to Improve	✔	Substantial Noncompliance	✔
(F) Evidence of prohibited discriminatory or other illegal credit practices								
▪ compliance with antidiscrimination laws and regulations	In substantial compliance		In compliance with substantive provisions		Not in compliance with substantive provisions		In substantial noncompliance	
▪ violations and corrective action	N/A		Nonsubstantive; promptly corrected		Substantive violations on isolated basis; violations may be repeated from previous exams		Demonstrates pattern or practice of prohibited discrimination or committed large number of substantive violations; violations may be repeated from previous exams	
V. Community Development **(H) Participation, including investments, in local development and redevelopment projects and programs**								
▪ awareness of programs	Thoroughly aware		Generally aware		Limited awareness		Unaware of or ignores programs	
▪ level or frequency of participation in programs	High level of participation, often in leadership role		Periodic participation		Rarely seeks out or participates		Little or no effort made to participate	
(K) Ability to meet community credit needs consistent with institution's characteristics								
▪ role in development of projects to foster economic revitalization and growth	Leadership role		Generally supports projects		Limited role		Small, if any, role	
▪ level of contact with government and private sector representatives to identify community development needs and opportunities	Has established good working relationships		Informed others of interest and involved in some aspects of planning or implementation		Rare		Little or none	
(L) Participation in other activities not covered under other performance categories that bear on extent to which institution meets community credit needs	Engages in other meaningful activities		Demonstrates willingness to explore		Demonstrates willingness to consider only when approached		Exhibits little or no interest	